MW01707318

LIFE LESSONS LEARNED CLIMBING KILIMANJARO

Never Say *Never*

by Neville Joffe

bizwisdom

Foreword

I was born in Cape Town, South Africa, more years ago than I care to admit. After leaving school and completing my military training, I joined my father's cap-making business (caps as in what you wear on your head) and learned the art of hat and cap making. While being street smart, an excellent business man, gutsy, moral and successful, my father was not an educated man and didn't believe in formal education. He believed that the best education I could get was to join his business. So I did, and I learned the business from the ground up, from sweeping the floors to learning how to cut and sew, create patterns, keep track of stock, and manage sales—the "whole nine yards."

A few years after I joined the business, we purchased a small factory about 300 miles outside of Cape Town that made knitted caps (toques) and scarves for the football market. The company used domestic knitting machines and the process was highly labour intensive. My dad saw the potential of the business if it could be commercialized. He suggested that my brother Alan continue running the cap factory with him and that I learn the knitting business. I took on the project with enthusiasm and soon learned how much I didn't know. After much trial and error, research and tenacity, I got the business on solid ground and we moved it to our premises in Cape Town. Once relocated, we purchased new industrial equipment and modernized the process. I spent months learning how to operate the new machines by visiting the machine makers in Syracuse, NY, in Florence and Milan, Italy, and in Osaka, Japan. I eventually built the company into a business that also specialised in knitwear for infants and young children. During this time I realised how deficient I was in formal business administration and decided that it was never too late to learn. I signed up for accounting courses at night school and subsequently acquired various other business qualifications through my studies. It was hard work to run a business during the day, study after hours and make time to spend with my young family in the evening.

In 1989 I moved to Toronto with my wife Marion and three sons to join a vertical manufacturing company that made sports uniforms for hockey, baseball, basketball and various other sports. A vertical manufacturer means that a factory produces all the processes instead of buying them in. Our factory produced the fabric from raw cotton and polyester, cut and sewed garments and decorated them with screen printing and embroidery. We even did all our own art work for our catalogues. The factory had been established in the 1960s and, while it had been traditionally very profitable, it was facing some financial problems. When I joined the company, it employed about 400 unionised people. I could only afford to buy a minority stake in the business with a promise that I would acquire more equity as the business became more profitable. I worked hand in hand with the founder, who was a generation older than me.

As part of the turnaround process I adopted an assortment of initiatives including Just In Time Inventory (JIT), Lean Manufacturing, The Theory Of Constraints (TOC), Total Quality Management (TQM), Balanced Scorecard, and Quality Circle. I have read literally hundreds of books and articles on these and other topics and continue to do so to this very day.

In 1994, North America was facing tough times. Interest was in double digits and inflation was still rife while we were entering the free trade era. Consumers refused to pay higher prices and many businesses went broke. During that time our unionised workforce was making demands on the company that would have bankrupted us, so I negotiated a wage freeze in support of a profit-share program. Since our staff members were skilled in the manufacturing process and not in finance, I started teaching small groups of people how they could improve profitability while making bonuses for themselves. I found it impossibly difficult because I was teaching them the same way that I had learned it and they just could not grasp the concepts. I even tried retaining the services of a consultant who specialised in teaching non-financial people the principles of accounting, but regretfully all she succeeded in doing was teaching the wrong thing more efficiently. The materials made simple concepts overly complicated and ineffectively connected the lessons to the practical implications of personal and business financial management.

I then tried a very non-traditional approach to teaching these concepts. I cashed $1,000 in small bills and crumpled them into a plastic garbage bag. I assembled all the staff in a room and then poured the crumpled bills onto a table. "This is called revenue," I said. I placed a handful of cash in a bucket and labelled it "wages." I continued the exercise with different buckets labelled "material," "rent," "maintenance," and "insurance," and then started tearing up $20 bills and throwing them into a bucket called "waste." The employees were silently shocked when I tore up the bills. "Why are you so surprised?" I asked. "You do this every day but just don't see it."

At the end of the demonstration, some cash remained on the table. I said, "What is left lying on the table is called profit." I shifted some of the remaining cash towards the crowd and said, "This is for all of you for your special hard work performed this year. The remainder is for the owners in return for all the financial risk they take to support this business." The group was stunned, and they finally understood the message I was trying to deliver. As a result of this initiative, key financial metrics dramatically improved; inventory levels decreased, accounts receivable were collected faster, low margin products were eliminated, and unprofitable customers were turned away.

It's important to know, however, that my business partner—being of the "old school mentality"—was vehemently opposed to my open-book philosophy, resulting in bitter arguments. He did not believe in training and insisted people should just do as they were told. Yet I was so sure that my approach had me on the right track to make the company even more profitable that I persevered and against all odds was able to successfully implement the concept. It was at that time that I discovered my true passion for teaching.

In 1997, after some disagreements about my future with the business and a dramatic difference in our leadership style, I sold my interest in the company back to my partner and founded AME Learning, a business that teaches financial literacy. I created an award-winning, patented, and interactive game-like tool to teach accounting and finance and have been using it to train non-financial professionals since 1998. The business has since grown to include a publishing division that uses the same patented platform for college and university curricula, and I have since written five leading textbooks on the subjects of accounting and finance that is used in conjunction with the technology.

During the past 35 years I have learned about the importance of business and personal relationships, the hardships of immigration, the dynamics of running a family business, the merits of education, the rewards for doing what I believe to be right even when all odds against me, living with the pain of broken promises, holding on to my integrity, and the true meaning of tenacity.

In 2010 I climbed Mt. Kilimanjaro. Why? Because I wanted to, because it's there, and because I love a challenge. More importantly, I wanted to do this while I had the physical strength and desire. The clock can never be turned back and I never want to find myself saying "I wish I did." As I was on the journey I had lots of time to think and I found it amazing how so many experiences on the mountain related to the experiences I have had in my life. This book uses the story of the climb to illustrate the many principles that I passionately believe in and that I want to share with you.

Thanks for coming on this life journey with me. I hope that you not only learn some life lessons and innovative business approaches but especially that you enjoy celebrating each day and each milestone in your life.

—Neville Joffe

Before everything else, getting ready is the secret of success.
—Henry Ford

One

Be Prepared

"What are you thinking?" asked Marion, my wife of 33 years. This statement was preceded by a glass (or two) of excellent Merlot at a dinner party held by my friend Allen and his wife Jill. During our conversation, Allen mentioned that he had always wanted to climb Mt. Kilimanjaro and hoped to realise this dream before his 60th birthday, which would be the following year. However, he didn't want to undertake this without friends and was looking for some volunteers to join him. Without hesitation, I piped up and said what a good idea I thought it was. I was assembling my "bucket list" and thought that this would be an excellent addition. Before my mouth closed, our friend Bernie had also blurted out, "I'm in." Given that Bernie was a triathlete and used to extreme exercise, he seemed a natural candidate—I'm not quite sure how his wife Ann felt about this, but she was quite silent.

Within a few days, Allen was all over the planning and was already finding tour companies in Tanzania that would take us. After some conversation with a few of our other friends, we assembled two others to join us, Bernard and Mario. We were now five in number and ready to go, or so we thought.

We researched various websites and decided to take the Umbwe route, which is the most difficult but the most unused and scenic route. We were told by many who had done this route that it's not for sissies, which started getting me a bit worried. While I don't consider myself a sissy, I'm not 20 years old any longer and, given that this was told to me by several fit young people, I was starting to doubt myself. Whenever I mentioned this adventure to any of my friends or family, I kept getting the same answer: "What are you thinking?" or "Leave it to the youngsters." I am somewhat of a stubborn individual, however, and the more I heard these negative comments, the more determined I became to go ahead.

At the time of making the decision I weighed 190 pounds and, while I did go to the gym occasionally, I was far from being fit enough to take on an adventure like this.

I started working out on a regular basis, focusing on the stair climbing machine (murder), the steep gradient treadmill, and lots of upper leg strengthening. (If someone tells you that you don't need to train for Kilimanjaro, tell them they are talking nonsense. I was thankful for all the training and it was worth every drop of sweat.) I also attended a weight-loss clinic which counselled me on the merits of healthy eating and how to manage a lifestyle that includes balanced diet and exercise. Within seven months, my weight was down to 162 pounds and I FELT GOOD. And I could tell I was getting into shape because it was nice for a change not to ask myself, while tying my shoelaces, what else I could do while I was down there.

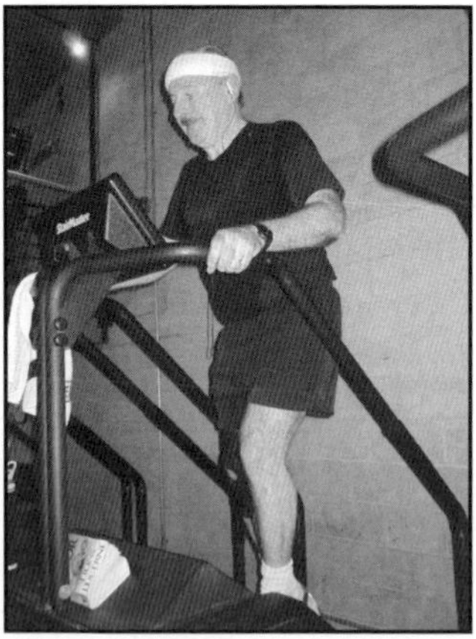

We were also guided as to what to buy for the trip. The list was exhaustive and included various levels of clothing, which were important to ensure that we were prepared for the extreme climates—ranging from very hot and humid at the base to sub-zero temperatures at the top, and everything in between. The boots were the most important item on the list. In fact, we were told that we should travel with our boots in the plane in case our bags went missing. Clothing can be replaced, but there is no substitute for well-worn-in boots. Customs and immigration must have thought we were nuts!

Our clothing included undershirts and socks that wick away moisture. We were told that freezing perspiration is a bad idea in cold climates. We also needed extra layers for the evenings and very warm down clothing for the summit. I have included the full list of requirements below; you may find it useful should you decide to embark on this type of extreme altitude adventure.

Item	QTY	Comments
OFFICAL PAPERS		
Valid passport and visa		
International health card with immunizations		Tanzania is a yellow fever–infected area and requires that you have had an immunization before entering the country.
Travel and medical Insurance		
Money		U.S. dollars (cash) or traveller's cheques.
TRIP ESSENTIALS		
Gear (duffel) bag	1	+/- 80 litres for transporting gear.
Daypack	1	Between 20 and 35 litres. Large enough to carry your camera, water, raingear, snacks and warm clothing.
Small lock	2	To lock the zippers together.

Continued

Item	QTY	Comments
FOOTWEAR		
Hiking boots	1	Waterproof, ankle height and **well worn in.**
Walking shoes	1	Comfortable, lightweight shoes.
Gaiters	1	Durable and preferably waterproof to protect against mud.
Warm socks	2	For use higher up on the mountain and in colder weather.
Trekking socks	5	For the lower slopes of Kilimanjaro.
Liner socks	2	To be worn under warm socks in case of extreme cold.
OUTERWEAR (THIRD LAYER)		
Outer trousers and jacket	1	Waterproof, breathable, and windproof.
Raincoat or poncho	1	
INSULATION (SECOND LAYER)		
Fleece jacket	1	Polar fleece 300 or a Polar fleece 100 and 200 (equal to a 300 series).
Fleece pants	1	Polar fleece pants.
NEXT TO SKIN (FIRST LAYER)		
Thermal underwear pants	1	Polar fleece is best.
Thermal underwear tops	1	Polar fleece is best.
Underwear		Wickable and breathable fabrics are ideal.
CLIMBING ACCESSORIES		
Beanie and scarf or balaclava	1	Polar fleece is best.
Liner gloves	1	Polypropylene liner gloves.

Continued

Item	QTY	Comments
Outer gloves	1	Waterproof, windproof, and breathable.
Hat	1	With a wide brim.
Trekking poles / walking sticks	2	Good quality and adjustable.
Insulated water bottles	1	**Compulsory** to stop water from freezing high up on the mountain.
Water bottle	2	Any leak-proof bottle in a pouch.
Headlamp	1	Popular models are the Energizer headlamps.
Water purification tablets	40	Chlorine or iodine based.
Sunglasses and clear goggles if climbing via Arrow Glacier	1	Good UV-protected lenses.
Batteries and spare bulbs	8	For headlamps and other devices.
Hand warmers	4	Optional.
Multi-tool (e.g., Leatherman)	1	For those last-minute repairs and general jobs (optional).
Sleeping bag and inner lining	1	Rated to at least -20°C.
Sack liner	1	To ensure that all your gear stays dry.
ACCESSORIES		
Hiker's towel	1	Compact and quick drying.
Toilet kit		Soap, toothbrush, toilet articles, nailbrush, handy wipes (wet wipes), etc. It is best to bring small, trail-size containers.
Toilet rolls	2	
Sunscreen lotion	1	Preferably oil-based SPF30+.
Vaseline		Avoid friction with your socks to prevent blisters.

Continued

Item	QTY	Comments
Lip balm	1	SPF rated is best.
Ziploc bags		To protect your camera, binoculars, etc., from dust.
Baby wet wipes		When you are far away from soap and water.
Rainproof bag covers		To protect your daypack from rain.
HIKING GEAR		
Trousers	1	Wickable, quick-drying, explorer-type fabric.
Casual shirts	2	For use before and after your climb.
T-shirts	5	For lower altitudes.
Regular underwear		
FIRST AID		
Personal first aid kit		Include painkillers and muscle rubs, Imodium (for diarrhoea), Valoid (for nausea and vomiting), Diamox (diuretic), and rehydration powder (potassium).
Insect repellent		This is malaria country.
Earplugs		You will hear every sound at night on the mountain and you will need your sleep.
Plastic bags		For dirty toilet paper between camps, to be discarded properly at the next camp.
Sense of humour		

We all bought our equipment at Mountain Equipment Co-op in Toronto because it was the only store that, besides having very knowledgeable staff, was prepared to take back products or swap any equipment that was not suitable. Case in point, I bought a very expensive pair of boots and after two months, I could not get comfortable in them. When I asked them if I could swap them for something else, there was no hesitation. The second pair was wonderful and became my best friend. I tried to return a pack of unopened batteries that my wife bought from another camping store because they were incorrect and they refused to take them back for a refund or even a credit. Guess which store I would choose to shop at again!

We trained for eight months and by the time we left Toronto on February 17, 2010, en route to Tanzania via Amsterdam, we were well prepared for the climb. (Tanzania is just south of Kenya on the east coast of Africa.)

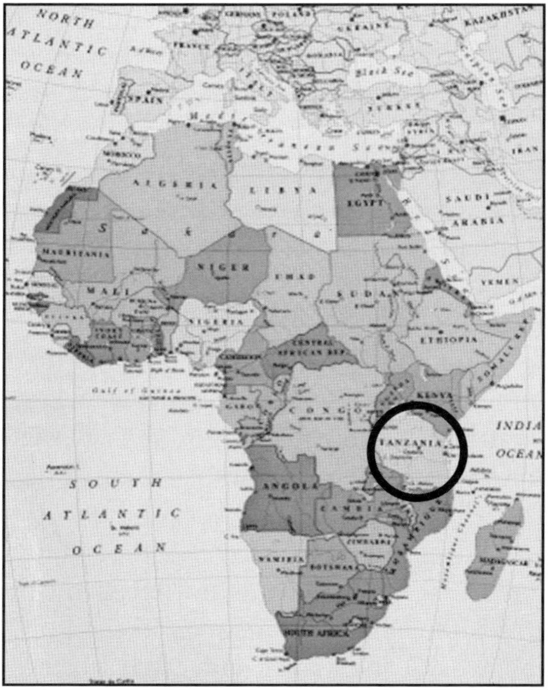

We arrived at Kilimanjaro airport after travelling 7 hours to Amsterdam, waiting a few hours in the airport, then flying another 10 hours directly to Kilimanjaro airport.

"The Five Musketeers" ready for a shower and a sleep.

We had a lot more helpers than bags.

Going through customs was an interesting experience. We were greeted by a "doctor" before collecting our bags. (Since he was wearing a white coat with a stethoscope around his neck, we thought it a reasonable assumption. Actually, if he had been wearing operating scrubs, he might have been even more convincing.) He requested us to fill in a form to say that we had been administered a yellow fever shot. He did not ask for ID. All we had to do was to sign a card with our name on it and hand it in.

We were then greeted by the friendly driver who had been sent to pick us up and take us on the 40-minute drive to our hotel. The moment we exited the airport, we were surrounded by people wanting to help us. It got so bad that the driver eventually had to intervene to fight them off. They all wanted tips for their help and we were uncertain how to manage this situation; we did not want to be antagonized but at the same time we felt uncomfortable and bothered by the constant swarming of people begging to help us in the hopes of getting paid for their work. The driver suggested that we give $2 to each helper and that we should give the money to him so that he could distribute it "at some later time." (This is probably more than they would earn in an entire day.) Since we felt that he may keep all the money for himself, we thought of a better plan. We all contributed a few one dollar bills and gave them to the helper who seemed the eldest and said he should distribute it. Since this was done in front of the rest of the group, we hoped that he would be quite fair in the manner in which the money was disbursed, failing which he would no doubt suffer the consequences from his peers.

Repacking my gear the night before the climb.

We spent the night at a humble but clean hotel which consisted of separate rooms that resembled cottages, and we enjoyed a simple meal together. Our guides spent a little while with us and explained how we should prepare for the next day's climb. We were to meet at 7:00 a.m. and after breakfast we were to store our extra baggage, which would be retrieved after the climb.

We were each allowed a maximum of 15 kilograms (about 32 pounds) in a tote bag that would be carried by the porters. We were well advised to pack everything in plastic Ziploc bags because of the likely event that it would rain during the first couple of days in the forest. We were really glad we did this. After checking all of our equipment and packing our daypacks, we enjoyed a good night's sleep.

The next morning we met for breakfast and watched the porters load the van that would take us on the 45-minute journey to the base of the mountain where we would commence the adventure.

Life's Lessons: Be Prepared

Planning in business is just like bringing a map when you're travelling. I know this seems trite but let me explain the benefits of planning. Have you ever watched the TV program called Shark Tank (or Dragons' Den in Canada)? If so, you will recall many instances where potential investees have stood in front of the "sharks" (investors) without having a business plan and without knowing their financial numbers or marketing strategies. These people are always sent on their way really fast (and without funding). Ever tried going to a bank for a loan without knowing your business numbers or plan? You will also be sent on your way really fast and without funding. Mapping out your business plan is no different than mapping out a route on a mountain. Getting lost can be very dangerous in either case. That being said, I am a very practical individual who does not believe in overkill. If you are in a small start-up business, you don't need to map out a plan with every tiny detail—mostly because few will come to pass as planned. However, you do need a business plan that includes the following at minimum:

- Expected sales with detailed planning of how you will support your sales assumptions (be brutally honest with yourself)
- Cost of sales (what does each sale cost, e.g., the cost of the product)
- Operating costs, including all fixed and variable costs
- Projected profits
- Cash flow (profits are not the same as cash flow)
- Ensure that the plan shows both the stretch target (be realistic but aggressive), the absolute minimum you should expect in sales, and the maximum you expect in costs

This is called a sensitivity analysis and it will help you be better prepared in case things do not go as planned (which is very common). No one likes surprises—especially not bank managers and financiers.

Maintaining Valuable Vendors

The story of the wonderful retailer that exchanged my boots is a great example of a memorable business experience. Such experiences are important if you want to build goodwill. Richard Branson of Virgin Airlines preaches this concept in all his business ventures. If you Google Richard Branson, you will find lots of quotes and great stories about his successes and failures and especially about his philosophy relating to the power of outstanding service. One theme which seems to encapsulate his general philosophy of business success is, "Focus on what people need and on how services and products can be improved to make them more practical, comfortable and enjoyable."

Over the past 35 years, I have learned that it's sometimes better to pay a reasonable premium for excellent quality or service rather than using a less expensive service to save a few dollars. The saving is not always worth it. When I was in the manufacturing industry, I learned this the hard way. I would often scout around for the least expensive vendor to dye our fabrics without focusing on quality and service as a priority. After being penalised to the tune of several thousand dollars for a late delivery to a retail chain because we received our fabrics late from a new dye house, we quickly reverted back to our old vendor who, while a little more expensive, always delivered on time. While on the topic of vendors, this brings me to my next point...

Leave Some Profit for Someone Else

I know lots of people who make sure to squeeze their vendors for every cent they can get. Guess what? While you may win in the short term, you earn no loyalty from your vendors in the long term—you will realize this fast if you ever need a favour.

The message? Leave some profit on the table for others. This does not mean that you should not negotiate hard and get the best deal when you can. It means that you should not exploit your vendors to the extent that they lose money on a deal and are only doing business with you because they are desperate. Vendors are no good to you when they are bankrupt and can no longer supply you.

If you mistreat your vendors, they will be acutely aware that you are abusing them and will feel no loyalty towards you. In fact, they will likely feel anger and resentment and be less likely to support you when you need them. For example, if you are in a situation where you need the goods urgently, they may be less co-operative or less willing to accommodate you.

I used to provide services to a large business that negotiated every cent, pushing me until I was just one last push away from turning the order down. As much as I needed the business, I knew that I was being exploited, so at last I graciously suggested to the owner that she buy her services from someone else who could accommodate her pricing needs.

Choose the Right Partners

Although we all got along well during the climb, I have heard of horror stories of people who have gone on various types of trips and had miserable experiences because of incompatible companions. Choosing the right partners, whether they are your financial partners or employees, is crucial to your success. I have had my fair share of bad experiences with incompatible partners and incompetent and dishonest employees. Bad partners and employees will suck all your energy from you and rather than complementing you and helping you build your business, they will compromise your ability to grow and might even destroy your business. Sometimes we think that our partner, employer, or employee is the right person except for one or two minor concerns, but minor concerns can end up as major concerns and spoil the relationship. I remember employing a bookkeeper whose quality of work was excellent except for one issue. Even though his work was always up to date, he would often come late to work or even not turn up for the entire day. This caused all sorts of problems. He was often not there when I needed him and, by allowing this behaviour, I was setting a precedent for my other employees that this was an acceptable practice. Even though I liked the individual and was happy with the quality of his work, I eventually had to fire him.

Another example relates to a business partner who started a business that I later bought into. While we had lots of common goals, enjoyed a common work ethic, and operated a fabulously profitable business, our management styles were completely different. This created huge stresses in our relationship, which affected the morale of the company's employees as well as our mutual health. I eventually sold my interest back to him and left the company. If you are an employee and are not happy at work, you are often better off seeking new employment. Stress is a killer—it damages morale, enthusiasm, and creativity and can seriously affect your health.

There is an expression which holds true to choosing partners: The whole should be greater than the sum of the parts. One and one should equal more than two. In other words, the combined efforts of you and your partner(s) should be greater than the sum of your individual efforts.

Summary of Learning Outcomes

Being prepared will eliminate significant stress in your life. This principle applies to both your personal and business life.

Choose the right partners. Sharing the same values is critical to the success of both personal and business relationships. In your personal life, partners can be regarded as your life partner and your friends. In business, partners can be regarded as your boss, work colleagues, customers, suppliers, and even your banker.

Using This Information to Improve my Life

In sequence of importance, list all the areas in your personal and business life where you think better preparation will benefit you in some way. For example, if you tend to routinely run late, write down some potential solutions and ways to improve (e.g., getting directions before you leave, allowing more time to get to meetings, planning where you should park). If you continuously run out of time when preparing for exams, identify ways to allow yourself sufficient time in the future. (See Chapter 4—Managing Expectations.)

____

____

____

____

____

____

____

List all those relationships that are not helping you achieve your goals. For example, try asking yourself the following questions. In your personal life, are your friends the type of people that provide you with the positive influence you need? If you are in business, is the job really what you want? Are you happy with the people with whom you work? Do your vendors provide you with the service you require? Are your customers sucking the life out your business? In sequence of importance, list all those partnerships that you need to change or influence.

Partners in my personal life

Partners in my business life

Expect the best, plan for the worst, and prepare to be surprised.
—Denis Waitley

Two

Prepare for the Unexpected

Day 1: We arrived at the base of the mountain after a very bumpy 45-minute drive in a Jeep. We were all geared up and anxiously anticipating the commencement of the climb. Mt. Kilimanjaro is a national park and requires that climbers register at

20 porters packing the food and equipment.

Signing the register at the base of the mountain

the base before they begin their journey. I guess they want to ensure that all the climbers return—although, considering that we never checked out after we came down, I don't know how they would monitor this. Be that as it may, it was interesting to flip through the registration book and see the names and ages of people from so many countries. Since the members of my group were all in our 50s we were older by far than the majority of the climbers.

We watched the porters pack the journey's supplies, which included an assortment of food, tents, mats to sleep on, and a long list of other equipment too numerous and diverse to mention. There were 20 porters and four guides to support the six of us. It appeared to be a lot of support but when one realises how much equipment and supplies are needed to support six people (plus the guides and porters) for seven days, one can see how it would be difficult to manage with less people. Each porter was not allowed to carry more than 15 kilograms (about 32 pounds) and so all the baggage was weighed on a scale before each porter loaded up.

There are six routes used to climb Kilimanjaro. (Each has different elements that can reasonably cause a climber to select one over the other.) There are routes that approach from the west, the north, and the south, and each offers different viewpoints. All of these routes are listed below. We used the Umbwe route, which is number 6 on this list.

1. **The Machame Route** is also known as the "Whiskey Route" in comparison to Marangu. This is because Machame is a more difficult route and does not have sleeping huts for accommodation. Machame is the second most popular route on the mountain.
2. **The Marangu Route** is also known as the "Tourist Route" and the "Coca-Cola Route." It is the most popular route and is considered "touristy," since it offers sleeping huts and beverages such as Coca-Cola along the way it. It is also the easiest route.
3. **The Rongai Route** is the only route that approaches Kilimanjaro from the north, near the Kenyan border. It is similar to Marangu.

4. **The Shira Route** is a difficult route that begins in the west. What is unique about Shira is that the first section of the trail is not hiked, but rather driven. Therefore, climbers using Shira will miss out on hiking through one of Kilimanjaro's ecological zones, the rainforest. Climbers will also miss out on a beautiful part of the climb since they will not see any of the wildlife that is otherwise evident in the first days of the climb.

5. **The Lemosho Route** is nearly identical to the Shira route described above, but with one notable difference: the first section of the trail is hiked. This schedule means that the Lemosho Route is a longer route, usually taking seven to eight days to complete.

6. **The Umbwe Route** is the least used, mostly untrafficked route on the mountain. This is for good reason; it is also regarded as the most difficult route on the mountain. Umbwe is a steep, constant, straight climb to the top. But it is mostly avoided because the ascent profile does not give climbers much time to adjust to the altitude. The success rate is very low. Umbwe is considered to be a very difficult, taxing route, and one that should only be attempted by strong hikers who are also confident of their ability to acclimatize to altitude. This is the route that we chose.

The terrain on the first day was green, lush and wet.

There was a steep pathway for the first few hours. The porters were seriously disorganised for our first meal experience.

The conditions on the first day were very tropical, hot, and humid (about 35°C) with heavy rain in the afternoon. Given that malaria is a serious threat in Tanzania, we were happy that we had mosquito patches and spray to ward off the little critters. Unbeknownst to us, one member of the group had not taken anti-malaria tablets before the climb. Not that he became ill, but by the end of the first day, we realized just how many mosquitoes we'd be dealing with and what danger he might be subjected to. We set off at about 10 a.m. The terrain was almost jungle-like with large amounts of foliage, thick and dense bush, lots of mud, and a very damp atmosphere. There was a permanent audible buzz in the air which was a refreshing reminder to keep applying mosquito repellent.

The trek started off with a flat, artificially made path. We were all joking around that this was a "real walk in the park" and wondering why people made such a big deal of the climb. Within an hour or so, we had changed our opinions as the gradient

I was ill-prepared for heavy rain.

became noticeably steeper. The challenge was made more difficult due to a combination of the gradient's increase, jet lag, the heat, and the altitude. At about 1:00 p.m., the guide suggested that we stop for lunch, and immediately upon this announcement rain started pelting down in sheets. All hell broke loose while we scrambled to find our ponchos and cover up our knapsacks. It was at that time that I realised that the poncho I brought with me was totally inadequate. It leaked something awful and was not big enough to cover my backpack. I was soaked within 10 minutes. Plus, while the contents of our packs were stored for the most part in Ziplocs bags, we did not think to protect the outer layer of the large bags that were being transported by the porters.

The porters left supplies lying all over the path—it was a miracle that they could find anything. Surprisingly, though, they erected a tent in record time and used it to cook our meal. I guess they were organised in their own fashion. Lunch consisted of fried chicken, buns, and fruit. Clearly fresh food would have to be eaten first so it was anyone's guess what we were to eat for the next seven days. When the porters were ready to serve lunch, we heard a commotion and lots of yelling. We discovered that the porter who was in charge of supplies had forgotten our eating utensils. The chief guide was yelling in Swahili, the local language, so we had no idea what he was saying. Given the way the porter was shaking, we could only imagine what it might be. The chief guide explained what had happened and said that he had used his cell phone to call the base camp and let them know. (Cell phones actually worked on various parts of the mountain.) The porter would have to return to the base camp and pick up the utensils, which would be waiting for him there. This would take him about three hours one way and then he would have to turn around and catch up to us by nightfall. We felt really sorry for him having to hike an additional six hours.

We departed from our lunch stop at about 2:00 p.m. It did not take long for the porters to rush by us at probably twice the speed of our walking rate. The gradient was quite steep and by the time we reached the camp at 5:00 p.m. we were soaked to the skin with rain and sweat. We spent our first night in tents at Umbwe Camp, 5,500 feet (about 1,800 metres) above sea level—we were cold, shivering, and just a little miserable, wishing for our warm, cosy beds at home. The camp was situated among lots of trees whose roots were protruding through the ground—that evening we learned that sleeping on these roots was not the most comfortable situation. Had we known that the ground conditions would be so rough, we would have bought inflatable mattresses rather than using the thin foam ones supplied by the tour company.

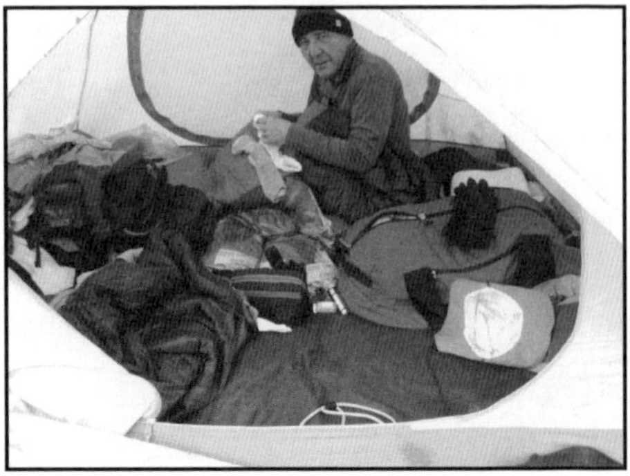

Bernard getting organised. Two adults in a small tent required some serious manoeuvring and patience.

After a restless sleep, we were awakened early and soon learned the importance of preparing our gear the night before. We had all assumed that it would not take too long to get dressed in the morning. Then again, none of us had ever had to share a 6 x 6 foot tent (2 x 2 metres) with another large adult, two sleeping bags, two large tote bags, and two large backpacks as well as other equipment. Luckily, we managed to organise ourselves so that the two large guys—Bernard and Allen—were buddied up with the two small guys, Bernie and me. Mario was the odd man out, and the last to join the group, so he had his own (very small) tent. I can't even imagine what it would have been like if Allen and Bernard (both over six feet tall) had shared a tent! It would have given a whole new meaning to the word "friendship."

As we tried to get ready on our first morning, it was common to unpack a piece of clothing, put it down, and not be able to find it again five minutes later. No, it wasn't dementia. It was about trying to organise our stuff without our spouses doing it for us. Army training in the 1970s did not prepare us for this. To exacerbate the tight ergonomics, everything was wet from the previous day's hike. All in all it was quite the challenge. From that moment onwards, we all learned the benefits of preparing everything the night before so that things would be less traumatic in the morning.

Once we were ready, we were each given a small plastic container filled with warm water, soap, and a dry cloth with which to wash. Given the low temperatures, this was no fun at all. We had to brave, not only the lack of amenities, but the cold as well. Oh, how we longed for our home comforts. Sometimes one takes basic luxuries for granted—but when one is deprived of them, one quickly learns to appreciate them.

Life's Lesson: Prepare for the Unexpected

On the first day of our hike, I was ill-prepared for the rain, sleeping conditions, and getting organised for the next day. Not having the right poncho made me wet and caused me to feel chilled and miserable for hours. Not having the appropriate mattress caused a painful and restless night (and this was to be repeated for all seven nights of the trek). Not preparing my tote bag the night before caused all sorts of frustrations the next morning, resulting in me not taking some crucial supplies in my daypack for the next day's hike. That being said, my group and I had no way of anticipating these issues because we were never told to expect them by the tour company. Were they wrong? Of course, but pointing it out would not help our situation. Given that the tour company's employees are supposed to be experienced, they should have told us to expect rain, hard surfaces to sleep on, and tight ergonomics, and they should have guided us in packing our bags. The point, however, is that life is full of surprises and one should always be adaptable to change. While one cannot anticipate what the change will be, we should be mentally prepared to accept and embrace it.

So, how does this principle apply to a business?

If everything only worked out according to plan we would all be far better off in so many ways. Consider the following scenarios in your personal life:

- You lend money to a friend who fails to pay you back when promised.
- You thought you would get $5,000 for your car but ended up only getting $4,500.
- The holiday that you planned was supposed to cost you $1,200 but ended up costing $1,500 because you forgot to add the taxes.
- You lost your job due to budget constraints in the company.

The list includes just a few of the endless types of things that can go wrong in your personal economic life. This is even truer in a business environment. Consider these examples:

- You thought the customer would buy your product but they changed their mind at the last moment. In the meanwhile, you were so convinced that the product would sell that you already bought and paid for the product, which was made especially for your customer.
- The bank said that the approval of your loan application would be contingent upon you getting a deal that seemed a sure win. However, at the very last moment the

loan's officer changed his mind because the seemingly guaranteed deal did not happen. In the meanwhile you had already hired someone based on the loan.

- You sold a product to a customer on credit terms and she went bankrupt. Your ability to pay your supplier was dependent on the collection of the money.

Again, this list of "hard luck" stories could be endless. Fortunately there are ways to help manage these expectations.

Here are some key principles that you should know.

- Plan for the worst-case scenario by using the "**if-then principle**." Let's test this principle with the examples used above.
- **If** the customer changes his mind, **then** I will have a financial problem. **If** I don't buy the product before the customer pays me up front, **then** I will have no risk.
- **If** the bank does not approve the loan, **then** I will not hire a new person. **If** I don't hire the new person, **then** the business may not be able to grow at the desired rate but I will not have a financial problem.
- **If** the customer goes bankrupt, **then** I will have a major financial crisis. **If** I get money up front or the appropriate guarantees that I will be paid, **then** I will be in good financial shape.

The if-then principle can help you prepare for the worst-case scenario, and this will help you build a contingent plan in case of everything going wrong. FEAR is an acronym for False Evidence Appearing Real, which I will expand upon later. It's very stressful not knowing what's ahead but predicting what the outcome might be by considering the risks and planning for them will reduce your risk of failure while significantly decreasing your stress levels. **In other words, failing to plan is planning to fail.**

Here are some more examples of how you can reduce stress by preparing for the unexpected in your personal life. (Try applying the if-then question to each of these examples and you will see the wisdom of planning for the unexpected.)

- Always be sure to have sufficient gas in your car.
- Keep your keys in the same place at all times so you don't have to go searching for them.
- Take out your clothes the night before—you never know if you might oversleep and miss an important appointment.
- If you have to wake up for an important meeting or an exam, use two or more alarms. You never know when one will fail to wake you up.
- Leave plenty of time to get to your appointments. Traffic might hold you up or you could have a flat tire on the way.
- If you are taking a flight, leave plenty of time in your schedule for unexpected delays.

Summary of Learning Outcomes

1. Prepare for the unexpected.
2. Mentally prepare yourself for the likelihood that you will need to adapt to a change in plans.
3. Can you live with the consequences of a decision? Apply the if-then principle.
4. Don't take basic luxuries for granted.

Using This Information to Improve my life

List situations in your life where you think you can take some risk without being sure of the possible outcome. Apply the **if-then principle** and create a plan to reduce your risk or at the very minimum be prepared for the outcome. Examples:

If I don't have a cash flow forecast, **then** I might run out of cash. Action: I need some help to create a spreadsheet so I can plan the cash flow needs of my business.

If I start studying for a test next week instead of this week, **then** I will probably have to study next weekend and cram during the week. Action: Start studying now so I can have some reserve time left for other unknowns. I can put on hold my other projects that are not as urgent.

"The difference between a successful person and others is not a lack of strength, not a lack of knowledge, but rather a lack of determination."

—Vince Lombardi

Three

It's Tough on the Way Up

Senicio trees that look like giant pineapples.

Day 2. We left camp at 8:00 a.m. after eating breakfast, which consisted of boiled eggs, toast, peanut butter, and honey. We headed out for Barranco camp, a very long hike which took us most of the day. Eating protein and carbs at the beginning of the day was really important to ensure that we were adequately

At times the slope was 45 degrees.

fuelled up. Despite the rain, our moods were not dampened because each mile was more interesting than the last. We saw giant-size cacti-like plants and incredible views of distant mountains shrouded by low-hanging clouds. As we moved higher, the temperature was noticeably cooler.

We were not quite prepared for the serious inclines throughout this part of the climb. There were times when we were rock-scrambling at a 45-degree angle. Bernard and Allen are over 6 feet tall and had the ability to reach upwards with their long legs and get a good toe-hold on the mountain side. Bernie and I are a little more vertically challenged and found ourselves needing help quite often, having to ask those ahead of us to give us a helping hand.

We arrived exhausted (despite the smiles] at Barranco camp in the late afternoon with the sun already setting. As usual, the porters had gone ahead of us to set up camp and prepare our food. We were always served a snack upon arrival that consisted of French fries or French toast, "pizza" or another high-carb food. The creativity of the chef always amazed us. For example, after a couple of days, once-fresh bread became French toast and finally, as it became increasingly more stale, it was served as Melba toast.

We were also amazed at how our porters managed to carry 32 pounds (15 kg) on their heads and charge ahead wearing only the most basic of clothing and shoes while we huffed and puffed despite wearing all our fancy gear. We kept remarking on this particular observation and how much people seem to think that one's success is reliant on fancy gear and equipment. These simple folk proved the point that wants and needs are quite different. They are living proof that so much can be done with so little.

By the end of Day 2, we had reached 12,000 feet (3,940 metres). High altitudes can do strange things to one's body. Perhaps this is a good time to take a minute and talk about this.

Porters carrying loads up to 32 pounds on their heads.

What Is Regarded as High Altitude?

High: 2,500 to 4,000 metres (8,000–13,000 feet)
Very High: 4,000–5,500 metres (13,000–18,000 feet)
Extremely High: over 5,000 metres (over 18,000 feet)

What Is Altitude Sickness?

It is difficult to determine who may be affected by altitude sickness. Simply put, some people get it and some people don't. Surprisingly, it has nothing to do with fitness. Most people, however, can ascend to 2,500 metres (8,000 feet) with little or no effect.

Altitude sickness can occur in some people as low as 8,000 feet (2,500 metres), but serious symptoms do not usually occur until over 12,000 feet. Even then it is not the height that is so dangerous; rather it is the speed with which you ascend to that altitude. Altitude sickness is actually more common in fit young men because they are more likely to attempt a rapid ascent by racing up the mountain like some indestructible super hero! As a general rule, it is far safer (and more enjoyable) to avoid altitude sickness by planning a sensible itinerary that allows for gradual acclimatisation to altitude as you ascend. You can race back down as fast as you like, as long as you don't break your neck!

The causes of altitude sickness are quite technical and can be read about if you do a little research on the Internet. Suffice it to say that it is caused by a lack of oxygen caused by improper acclimatisation, which can lead to potentially serious, even life-threatening altitude sickness. In addition to altitude sickness, climbers can experience Cheyne-Stokes respiration and acute mountain sickness.

Cheyne-Stokes Respirations

Individuals can experience this symptom at altitudes above 3,000 metres (10,000 feet). For most people, it is experienced as periodic interruption in breathing while they are sleeping. During the period when breathing stops, the person often becomes restless and may awake with a sudden feeling of suffocation. This type of breathing is not considered abnormal at high altitudes.

Acute Mountain Sickness (AMS)

AMS is very common at high altitude. Over 75 percent of individuals can show mild symptoms at altitudes over 3,000 metres (10,000 feet). The occurrence of AMS is dependent upon the elevation, the rate of ascent, and the individual. Many people will experience mild AMS during the acclimatisation process. The symptoms usually start 12 to 24 hours after arrival at reaching this altitude and begin to decrease in severity around the third day.

The symptoms of **mild AMS** include headache, nausea and dizziness, loss of appetite, fatigue and shortness of breath.

The best test for **moderate AMS** is to have the person walk a straight line heel to toe, just like police will ask a driver to do when they suspect him of drinking too much. Someone with moderate AMS would be unable to walk a straight line. This is a clear indication that an immediate descent is required.

Severe AMS includes a severe increase in the symptoms listed just above. It can cause an inability to walk, a decrease in mental status, and fluid build-up in the lungs. If a person suffering from severe AMS does not descend immediately, he or she could experience severe brain damage.

Another dangerous condition is called high altitude pulmonary edema (HAPE) which is a result of fluid build-up in the lungs. It causes all sorts of problems too graphic and gory to explain in detail. But you get the point.

Here are some basic and important guidelines for the prevention of AMS:

- Acclimatise slowly. If you go above 3,000 metres (10,000 feet), only increase your altitude by 300 metres (1,000 feet) per day, and for every 900 metres (3,000 feet) of elevation gained, take a full day's rest to acclimatise.
- Climb high and sleep low! You can climb high during the day as long as you come back down and sleep at a lower altitude.
- If you begin to show symptoms of moderate altitude sickness, don't go higher until symptoms decrease.
- If symptoms increase, go down!
- Eat a high-calorie diet while at a higher altitude.
- Staying properly hydrated is crucial because acclimatisation is often accompanied by fluid loss, so you need to drink lots of fluids (4–6 litres per day).
- Avoid tobacco, alcohol, and certain prescription drugs (check with your doctor).

I will address this potentially lethal condition later on again.

Life's Lessons: It's Tough on the Way Up

Does the idea of falling prey to altitude sickness scare you? It should because climbing too quickly can kill you. I have expanded on this problem for a reason.

People in business can fail for a host of reasons. I have trained and advised thousands of people in small businesses. The reasons for failure and for the severe stress the owners can experience are endless. There are, however, just a few key root causes behind most of the issues that challenge a stressed business owner. I will highlight two key causes here.

Too Proud to Seek Help

We all needed help on the climb. In fact, there were times on the climb that our lives could have been in danger had we not accepted help. Help included visiting a doctor who specialised in extreme altitude climbs. He advised us on what and what not to do. We sought advice from our tour company on what to take with us on the trip. (Okay, so it did a lousy job of that one!) We had lots of advice from the experts at Mountain Equipment Co-op who gave us suggestions about the best choice of clothing and supplies, which saved us a lot of time and money. We had help from the porters who carried our excess baggage, and we were given many tips from our guides along the way. Being in a job or operating a business is tricky at best and most people need help at one time or another. Unfortunately, egos often get in the way and people feel too proud to ask for help. There are many resources available, and many of them are available at no cost. Consider the following free resources:

- Books from the library
- Internet
- Friends
- Family
- Banking advisers

Patience

"Are we there yet?" Ever heard this before? Impatience can be dangerous. Think of some personal examples where impatience could actually kill you or someone else. For example, being in a hurry and running a red light, or walking too fast on a slippery surface. We faced similar dangers on the climb. Sometimes the rock surfaces were really slippery and we had to move at a snail's pace to prevent ourselves from being hurt. We had to make sure that our boots and climbing poles were securely positioned before taking our full weight up to the next level. Business is no different. Many business owners are in such a hurry to get to the next level that they mess up. Consider some of the following examples:

- Selling a product that still has quality issues.
- Hiring a person without taking the time to check her references.
- Selling to a customer without first ensuring that he is credit worthy.
- Buying products or services without taking the time to ensure that they will deliver what they promise.
- Expecting people to perform without taking the time to train them properly.

The list is endless, but you get the point. Orange trees flower in the spring time, and start to fruit shortly after that. Harvest occurs around the end of autumn or at the start of winter. Nothing you can do can accelerate this process. It's the law of nature. This same principle applies to many aspects of your personal and business life. I know it's tough when you are working on a new venture, whether it's your own business or you're building a career. You may feel anxious, wanting things to move ahead more quickly than they are. Be patient.

When patience was handed out, I was not first in line. I have been impatient all my life, and the older I get the less patient I tend to be. However, the climb up the mountain gave me a whole new perspective on patience and caused me to mellow. Here are some of my takeaways that I learned on the climb (mostly from the guides) and upon reflection when I returned and started writing this book.

- **Pole-pole** means slow-slow in Swahili, the local language of Tanzania. All the curio shops and stalls selling tourists stuff included T-shirts, hats, and other paraphernalia that read Pole-pole. It's a Tanzanian/Kilimanjaro mantra. Why? Because unless one adheres to this rule, you will stand little chance of summiting Kilimanjaro. The message? TAKE IT SLOW!
- **Understand others.** Imagine if our guides had been impatient when explaining how to avoid a critical life threatening situation such as how to ascend the Great Barranco Wall (Chapter Four). By us NOT understanding what needed to be done, we could have been seriously hurt or even killed. There is an expression that I use when training trainers in my business. Those who have a lot of knowledge forget what it's like for someone else to have little or no knowledge. I call this the Curse of Knowledge. Try empathising with others and you will see that you will exercise more patience. I will address this topic again in Chapter 6—Communication.
- **Create a realistic and clear step-by-step plan.** Earlier on I spoke about the importance of planning ahead and planning for the unexpected. By following these principles, you can learn to be more patient. There are very few plans that will work the first time exactly as they are written down. Be flexible and adjust the plan when necessary, and you will find your patience improving.

- **Take time out to think logically** about when you can realistically achieve your objective. In other words, take a break from your project to give yourself time to gather your thoughts. I learned this from riding a motorcycle. I have an awful sense of direction and being frustrated and having impatience on a motorcycle is really bad news! When I'm lost and feeling frustrated, rather than losing my patience, I stop my bike, gather my thoughts and work out the best plan to get to my destination one step at a time. Imagine if we were lost on the mountain! Being impatient would have made things worse.
- **Take it easy on yourself.** Things don't always turn out the way you want. My friend who didn't make it to the top was so very disappointed, but he knew in his heart that it was not his fault. He caught a stomach bug and became sick, and then the altitude got to him. There will be lots of times that you will not achieve your objectives on the way up. It does not mean that it's your fault. Imagine if a football player beat himself up every time he did NOT score! It's just part of "getting there."
- **Celebrate your accomplishments** when you achieve your objectives. Frequent small celebrations are a way to reward yourself for patience and to increase your motivation to be even more patient. More about this later.

Accept the setbacks. When we were summiting, we were walking at a very steep gradient on scree that was volcanic dust. It was so slippery that for every few steps we would take going up, it was easy to slip a few steps back. Slipping backward is bound to happen, whether it be in your studies, professional workplace, or personal life. We all have setbacks, hard lessons to learn, and disappointments to manage along the way.

Here is some background relating to Thomas Edison's invention of the incandescent light bulb in the late 1800s.

Edison realised that carbonised materials could be used for a filament that he wanted to use for the light bulb he was inventing. He tested the carbonised filaments of every imaginable plant and was even able to acquire fibers from places in the tropics. The experiments he performed were tedious but he never let up. In fact he was known to have tested more than 6,000 vegetable growths and kept contacting people in other parts of the world to find a substance that would work.

> "The electric light has caused me the greatest amount of study and has required the most elaborate experiments," he wrote. "I was never myself discouraged, or inclined to be hopeless of success. I cannot say the same for all my associates."

Genius is one percent inspiration and ninety-nine percent perspiration.

Before he died in 1931, Edison patented 1,093 of his inventions. Talk about patience!

> *"It's not that I'm so smart it's just that I stay with problems longer."*
>
> —**Albert Einstein**

Tap Tap Tap

Do you ever experience the following situations in your daily life?

- Tapping your feet while waiting in a line-up at the bank?
- Cursing because you have to wait your turn. even for a pleasant experience such as going to a movie?

- Sweating it out in traffic and honking your horn when in your heart you know that it won't help you get to your designation any faster?

I have no doubt that you can add a few more dozen irritating situations where you might lose patience, but here's a thought for you. There are times that I ride my motorcycle on long-distance trips and find myself in some weird places that don't even register on the GPS. On one trip, I headed down south towards North Carolina. When I reached Roanoke Virginia, I found myself winding through unknown streets, having to stop every so often to ask someone directions to my hotel. When I got back from the trip I was chatting to my friend Gadi in my bike club and told him about my frustrations of visiting strange cities and often getting lost. He said something to me that I never forgot. "Losing your patience on a motorcycle is dangerous. Don't worry about being lost because **you will always get to where you need to be.**"

Now, I lighten up, pace myself and keep my destination in mind and keep saying to myself: "I WILL get to the hotel tonight, so just relax."

That being said, I strongly believe that patience is a mental skill, one that can be practised and eventually mastered, even by the most impatient person.

On Losing Patience

When I'm stressed out, my back hurts, I get stomach cramps, and in general just feel lousy. I often feel this way when I become impatient as well. Impatience takes its toll on our bodies, because it generates stress, which elevates blood pressure and wreaks havoc with the body's internal organs and immune system. Impatient behaviour can strain relationships, cause discord in group situations, and can set a bad example in the workplace.

It is said that people who are impatient "have a short fuse." I once had a business partner who I can best describe as a person who had no fuse whatsoever. He would blow up at the slightest provocation, with no warning. He had no patience to sit through meetings, talk on the phone, or listen to suggestions. In general, he was just an intolerant man in every sense. His relationship with me and the rest of our staff was a permanent strain because we never knew when he would blow. I eventually left the company mostly because of the stress of being around him.

When you find yourself on the verge of losing patience, try adjusting your perceptions to the reality of the situation at hand. Don't work yourself into a lather for nothing. In short, learning patience is the surest way to accomplish your goals and dreams.

Summary of Learning Outcomes

1. No one ever said that achieving your objectives is always easy.
2. Don't be too proud to seek help. The most successful achievers have coaches and mentors.
3. Exercise patience. Great accomplishments don't happen overnight.
4. Create a realistic step-by-step plan to meet your objectives.
5. Celebrate success.
6. Accept your setbacks and don't be so hard on yourself.

Using This Information to Improve My Life

- List all those objectives that you wish to accomplish this week, month or in years to come. Break them up into short- and long-term goals.
- Identify those areas in which you need help and identify the resources that can provide the necessary help. For example, books, professional counselling, and focus groups.
- Create a realistic plan to achieve your objective (refer to the SMART principle in Chapter 5).

“Anger always comes from frustrated expectations”
—Charles F. Kettering

Four

Managing Expectations

Night of Day 2

That night I was so cold that I slept in three layers of clothing. I was also suffering from severe heart burn. I didn't know this at the time, but heartburn is a common ailment at these altitudes. Had I been warned of this, I would have brought antacid tablets with me. Given how tired I was and how much my legs hurt, I was looking forward to Day 3, which was considered a "rest day" to help acclimatise us to the altitude. Our expectation was that we would lie around the camp for a day and a night while playing cards, reading and generally relaxing while our bodies got used to the new altitude. We read about this concept during our research, which referred to Everest climbers who will often stay at a camp for weeks while their bodies adjust to the new altitude. We would be in for a rude awakening.

Day 3

When we woke up the next morning, we were surprised at how cold it was. Our gaiters (the covers over our ankles to prevent mud penetrating our boots) that we had hung over our tents were frozen solid. Staying clean was a painful experience at below-zero temperatures. As the saying goes, "We gotta do what we gotta do."

Washing up in sub-zero temperatures is not for sissies!

Our gaiters were frozen in the mornings.

At breakfast, the guides informed us that our acclimatisation "take it easy day" was a seven-hour hike to and from Lava Tower, volcanic rock that peaks at 4,642 meters (about 15,000 feet). They explained that climbing high today and sleeping low tonight would tell us if we could tolerate even higher altitudes or if we would show signs of altitude sickness. If we did show signs, we'd be okay as long as the symptoms subsided when we descended. If the symptoms continued, then our chances of making it to even higher altitudes were remote. It would also give us a chance to experience what a higher altitude would feel like, so there would be no surprises. Needless to say, the big surprise for us was the fact that we were doing this major hike at all.

We set out mid-morning, and the hike seemed to go on forever. It was cool throughout the day but clear and sunny. As we ascended, the landscape became more and more sparse with little greenery or life. Even birds of prey did not seem to fly this high. Our breathing became quite short and we were now getting a really "good" feel of what it was like to exercise at high altitude. I had a dull headache a few hours into the hike and took a Tylenol, which seemed to help. The other guys all suffered with the same symptoms.

It took a half a day climb to reach Lava Tower.

Lava Tower, 15,000 feet above sea level.

There were lots of peaks and valleys along the route, so we went up and down a lot. Every time we went down, we were always surprised that we had to climb up yet again. This continued for the entire day: going and coming back. When we reached Lava Tower, we stayed for about an hour to rest and hydrate. There was not much of a view from here other than lots of rocks and barren land.

We arrived back at Barranco Camp in the late afternoon absolutely exhausted. So much for a "rest day"! As usual, it was

There were lots of peaks and valleys during the 7 hour hike to and from Lava Tower. The landscape also became very barren.

very cloudy at this time of day, which meant we couldn't see our surroundings very clearly. Perhaps this was just as well, because we were in for another big surprise the next morning.

Day 4

We were awakened as usual at 7:00 a.m., washed up, had breakfast and were then briefed on the activities to expect on this fourth day. Our guide pointed to a rock wall a short way from the camp called the Great Barranco Wall. He told us very matter-of-factly that we would be climbing over the wall on our way to Karanga Camp, where we would sleep at an altitude of 4,681 meters (about 14,000 feet). He said that the hike would be very steep and very tough. We all looked at the wall in disbelief. It was incredulous that we were expected to climb

View of the Barranco Wall from the camp.

The Barranco Wall is a sheer rock face.

At times the gap between rocks was very narrow to navigate when ascending and descending.

over the wall without any rock-climbing experience and began protesting. Our guide simply shrugged his shoulders, as if to say "Sorry, but that's what you have to do, so suck it up!"

Fortunately for us, there were several other climbing groups leaving the camp at the same time as we were, so the large number of climbers, porters and guides meant we were forced to move really slowly. This gave us time to catch our breath and rest our weary limbs along the way when we needed to. At times, the rock surfaces along the pathways were so narrow that we had to hang on to the sides of the rock face with our fingers to ensure that we did not fall. It took us about three hours of arduous climbing to reach the top of the wall where the sites were wonderful. Alas, we did not have time to relax and take in the view because we had to keep moving if we were to reach the next camp before it got too dark. Karanga camp was much like Baranco except it was colder and more barren. Dinner comprised of "pizza" which was essentially stale bread topped with cheese and something

Karanga Camp was barren, misty and very cold. There was no evidence of plants or wildlife.

Porters carrying barrels of water.

that resembled tomato paste and vegetables. They "chefs" also fried potatoes and made French toast. For once in my life I had no conscience eating such high fat foods which was most welcome given our high calorie burn. The next day's hike to Barufu being the final camp before the summit was a relatively short 6 hour hike. We were already struggling to breathe and walk due to the altitude, so the hike was slower than the previous three days.

When we arrived at Barafu camp (4,600m / 14,000 feet) in mid-afternoon, it was misty and damp. It was a weird eerie feeling being so high up in the cloud. Our surroundings were lacking in colour consisting of mostly dull brown and grey with no greenery whatsoever. The group was quieter than usual because we were tired, cold and a little anxious. We did not know what to expect, especially since we could not see the summit above the clouds. There was no water at this altitude, which meant the porters had to bring up water in 20-litre (5-gallon) containers from a lower level. I felt so sorry for the porters who worked so hard for so little. Water was used very sparingly. There was just enough with which to make food for the evening meal and provide each of us with our 4-litre ration for the summit climb.

Life's Lessons: Managing Expectations

A Mt. Kilimanjaro ambulance.

The big issue for us on Day 3 and again on Day 4 was dealing with situations and circumstances that were different from what we had been told (and not told) to expect. It was not so much about the cold, the long hike or what was supposed to be a rest day, or about the long peaks and valleys that never seemed to end. It was more about having to deal with surprise after unpleasant surprise. I don't know of anyone who actually likes an unpleasant surprise. In fact I know of some people who don't like any kind of surprise, good or bad. These people like to know what to expect. Business is no different. The tour company that we chose to lead us on our climb of Kilimanjaro was a disappointment at best. The guides never volunteered interesting information about the geography of the area; they didn't have adequate safety equipment (their first aid kit could fit in your pocket); and they relied on cell phones, which limited reception unlike the two-way radios that other groups were using. I asked one of the guides what would happen if one of us were to have an accident. He said that if the accident happened at a higher level then we'd have to descend to a lower altitude where a special "ambulance" would meet us and then bring the victim down to a base camp. My perception of an ambulance was somewhat different to his interpretation. Take a look at the photo of the "ambulance" included here. I think I would sooner jump off the mountain than be taken down on one of those.

I have been asked on several occasions by people who want to experience the climb if I would recommend the tour company we used. Do you think that I would recommend them? Of course not. Even though they were a budget-conscious type of organization, I found out that a climber's safety could be compromised. That's not worth any bargain price. In the end, the company did not deliver what it said it would, which is why there were so many surprises.

In your personal life, you will earn significant credibility if you do what you say you will do. Business is no different. You will earn huge credibility if you do what you promise. Here are a few important examples.

1. If you promise a customer that you will deliver a product on March 20, then her expectations are that she will receive it on March 20 and not on April 10. When I was in the textile industry, we were always under pressure to deliver fabrics by a date that was sensitive to seasons. Even though the buyers were often slow in placing their orders, they still expected us to deliver on time. In other words, the industry had tolerated this practice for so long that the customers expected suppliers to move heaven and earth to deliver on time. I spent many sleepless nights worrying about how to deliver a product given the short lead time and eventually I began to turn down orders because I was losing credibility when I could not deliver according to my promise. This decision paid big dividends. Once I was in a position to persuade customers to place their orders earlier in exchange for guaranteed deliveries, I slept far better and made more money, because I did not have to pay late delivery penalties and staff overtime.
2. If you know that you will have a cash flow problem in a month's time (you know this because you monitor your cash requirements carefully), then you can warn

your bank manager of this short-term issue so that she knows you will be late in making a payment and she will not be surprised when it happens. This refers once again to having a map and a plan.

3. If you have made a promise to your partner, colleague, employer or employee and then realize you cannot honour the commitment, inform the individual the moment you know. By explaining the issue, and why you cannot deliver what you promised, you might create a positive outcome. I have no doubt that you can come up with many examples of having made a commitment that you could not deliver on for reasons beyond your control. When you manage the broken expectation, your stress will melt away.

Here are some tips that I've picked up along the way that can help you manage expectations:

Lighten up. In the previous chapter I mentioned the importance of lightening up when setting expectations. Expecting to climb Kilimanjaro in three days is an unrealistic expectation. Why? Because climbing at that rate of ascent is dangerous and certainly not doable for a person of my age. Your expectations must be reasonable, and they must be realistic. It is quite reasonable to assume that you will always have traffic, that your car may break down or the serviceman will arrive late. Expecting the world to run smoothly is like beating your head against the wall. Give yourself a break and lighten up. Have patience—it pays dividends.

How people perceive expectations of each other. How you perceive your performance may differ from how others perceive it. When I was told that Day 3 was to be a rest day, I took that as valid information and that became my reality. I internalised it and was mentally prepared for it. In other words, my reality was based on my perception. Why, then, did the guides not tell us ahead of time what to expect on Day 3? I wish I knew! Why did they waste our time and build up a false expectation? In business, when you run a campaign that is disguised as something else, you risk your credibility. Building up false expectations and not delivering on what you promise usually results in irreparable damage to your professional image, and sometimes the damage is beyond repair.

I have had my share of business relationships in which a colleague or partner has made promises and then failed to deliver, bringing a disappointing end to the relationship. There were usually excuses made such as "You didn't quite understand what I meant" or "Things changed, so I could not make good on the deal." I can list dozens of examples of people failing to deliver what they promised. On the flip side, I have to admit that I have made my fair share of commitments that I regretted later on because they were not realistic and I ended up being embarrassed that I could not fulfil my promises, thus causing hurt, disappointment, inconvenience or financial loss to my clients. In other words, my perception of the expectation was my reality and, when the reality did not turn out the way I thought it would, it ended up with unsatisfactory results.

You are who you are. How many times have you seen someone with something that you would like to have, such as a nice car, a fancy home, designer clothing. Perhaps you want to be like someone famous—an actor or an extremely successful entrepreneur like Bill Gates of Microsoft or Mark Zuckerberg of Facebook. Wanting these things is fine, but there is rarely a formula for "quick money." You have to earn it, and it takes time and patience. As the saying goes, "It's amazing how it takes 10 years to be an overnight success!" While quick success stories like Zuckerberg's are possible, they are a rarity and should not be used as an example of what is normal. In other words, you can allow other people to inspire you but you cannot be them. Just be yourself.

Managing Expectations in Your Personal Life

By Marion Joffe

Lift yourself up or weigh yourself down—the choice is yours.

Managing expectations is a tough human trait to deal with. Do we expect nothing but the best from others and then feel disappointed when these unrealistic expectations are not met? Or do we expect nothing from anyone, and feel elated when someone makes any small positive contribution?

One learns from experience, which is why that adage is so true: Wisdom is wasted on old age. My mother told me that it took her until she was 60 to realize that she had made a grave mistake: she expected others to have the same values, goals and expectations from others that she had.

So what's the answer, you ask? Rely upon yourself and don't expect too much from others. While it may sound cynical, it also makes you realistic and changes your approach towards others. A negative demeanour can cause others to sense your disappointment and dissatisfaction and make them miserable.

Allowing yourself to be governed by other people's lack of response, support or positive energy and feedback is setting you up for self sabotage. Setting high goals, be they inspirational, physical or financial, is essential to motivating you to get up each day. We should aspire to be the best that we can be, not necessarily "the best"!

Apathy is a rampant disease in today's society, especially with the new "me" generation wanting instant gratification without putting in the effort. Many people join clubs and organizations relating to their personal hobbies, but then expect everyone else to do the work and run the organization. The 80/20 rule applies. Twenty percent of the people do 80 percent of the work.

I recall a manager I worked for once asking me why I do "nice things" for other people. I said that I was inherently selfish because I was the beneficiary of the "giving" inasmuch as I derived immense joy and satisfaction from the giving.

Oprah taught a life lesson to many people when she began the "giving back" principal. She gave $1,000 to a group of people and asked them to come back in a few months demonstrating how the money worked had been used to benefit others. The stories were amazing and the results even more astounding. The principal was that effort can have a positive effect on other's lives. But not everyone has the effort or the inclination, so we should not expect it from them. Rather, we should be joyful when we receive an unexpected gift.

I felt so liberated and uplifted when I shed the burden of other people's expectations, be it work colleagues, family, friends or acquaintances. The choice is yours. Only you can help yourself to manage your expectations of others. Remember that human nature makes most people think of themselves first.

So pick yourself up, dust yourself off and wake up with a new approach to expectations. Trust me, your life will be far happier, and you may even be pleasantly surprised by the outpouring of positive energy you will receive.

Two More of Life's Lessons

1. Over Promise and Under Deliver

How many times have you had experiences relating to some of the following scenarios?

- "The best burger in town" turns out to taste like dog food.
- "The flight is scheduled to leave at 7:00 p.m." It leaves at 8:00 p.m.
- "Your new car is so economical that you will get 40 mpg." At best you cannot get better than 25.
- "You will receive your product within 5 business days or your money back." Yeah right! Try getting your money back after it arrived 10 days late.

- "Your new software is error free." Are you kidding me? There is no such thing. Errors are bound to crop up. It is an inevitable fact of life, so make it easier for yourself and expect it.
- "Our marketing services will help you double your sales." I would be ashamed to admit how many times I have fallen for these promises.

Do you feel a little angry by just reading the above failed promises even though some of them might not even have happened to you?

2. Under Promise and Over Deliver

- The plumber promises that the job will take no longer than 1 day and cost less than $500. He delivers in half a day and bills you $250.
- Going on vacation and experiencing bad weather. The hotel feels sorry for guests and provides free room movies for the day.
- When buying your new car, the salesman includes free floor mats, 5 free wash tickets and a full tank of gas.
- A restaurant offering a surprise of free deserts for your birthday.
- You had to wait an inordinate amount of time for your meal at a restaurant. Not only did the manager take off 50% from the cost of the meal but offered a free drink the next time you visit.

How do you feel after reading about these positive experiences? Good? It's interesting how one's state of mind changes when having positive versus negative experiences.

There are a few companies in the world today that will deliver on what they promise they will. If you were to buy an iPod, iPhone or any other Apple product, do you believe that you would get what was promised? Perhaps even more?

The result? At the time of writing, Apple is the most valuable company in the world. Why? Because it EXCEEDS expectations.

Summary of Learning Outcomes

1. Manage expectations by being candid.
2. Lighten up on yourself by setting reasonable expectations. Not everything in your life can be controlled.
3. Under promise and over deliver.
4. Be sensitive to expectations. Everyone has different values.

Using This Information to Improve My Life

List all those times where you have made a commitment to someone and failed to deliver.

Then list all those expectations that you are likely to make in the short and long term and adjust them to a level where you know for certain you have under promised and will likely over deliver. If appropriate, use the SMART principle in Chapter 5 to map out how you will deliver the expectations according to your promise. Here are a couple of examples to help stimulate your thoughts.

1. You promised your boss that you will sell $20,000 worth of product this month but you know that this is unlikely to happen. How would you revise your expectations so that you can deliver on your guarantee?
2. A long-time friend of yours could not drive for medical reasons and asked you to pick him up and drop him off at work each day. After three months of this service, when he recovered and began driving himself again, he never sent you a gift or even a card to say thanks. You cannot stop thinking about this and your animosity towards him is eating you up. Given that your expectation has not been met, how will you deal with this and how will you prepare your mind in the future for events similar to this?

Powers you never dreamed of. You can do things you never thought you could do. There are no limitations in what you can do except the limitations of your own mind

—Darwin P. Kingsley

Five

Keep the Vision in Mind

Evening of Day 4 : The Summit

Barafu Camp is a barren, dry, lifeless and uninviting place. Other than our presence, there was no sign of either plant or animal life. While it was a little eerie, it was also somewhat peaceful. The balance of the afternoon was spent checking our day packs and just hanging around chatting with one another and with climbers from other groups. Anxiety had set in and we were all joking about our expectations. Secretly though, our group all had mixed feelings about the last part of the trip, which was about to commence in a few short hours. Given that there was no water supply at that altitude, the porters had to go back and forth from a stream about an hour from the camp, making the climb as they carried 20-litre barrels on their heads. We had an afternoon snack of fried potatoes and soup. It was

Barafu Camp is a cold, barren, dry, lifeless and uninviting place.

Leaving Barafu for our destination: the summit. Notice the headlamps.

very cold, so the high-carbs and hot soup went down really well. At about 7:00 p.m. we were told to try and get some rest because we would be awakened at 10:00 p.m. for some food before we began the summit climb at 11:00 p.m. No one was speaking, needless to say, and neither could we sleep. I was very anxious and excited all at the same time. Not knowing what to expect, we began to mentally prepare ourselves for the unknown.

We were "awakened" at 10:00 p.m. as promised. We each got dressed in three layers of clothing, checked our gear and packed our own food for the climb, which consisted of trail mix, protein bars, small Bar One Chocolates (easy to eat and high in calories). We were given hot tea and biscuits, and then, after checking our headlamps, we were divided into two groups of three climbers each. Two guides stayed in front and two guides followed from the back. All the porters stayed behind to await our return to base camp.

It was a beautiful clear evening with the full moon shining bright. Although our vision was limited, we could still see the headlamps of the other groups ahead of us. The guides were singing and chanting in Swahili, which helped us fall into a well-paced walking rhythm. There was very little talking. Each hour, we stopped to hydrate and eat a bit. We would also check our pulse to ensure that we were not working too hard and check on each other to make sure that we were lucid and that there was no sign of altitude sickness. Looking after each other was crucial. The gradient was extremely steep (40–50 degrees in parts) and we just plodded along one small step at a time in the darkness of the night.

We were using Camel Packs to store water. These packs are stored in the backpack and can hold about 4 litres (1 gallon) of water. There is a plastic pipe which runs from the backpack to a mouthpiece in the front from which to suck water while walking. The water that remains in the exposed piece of plastic pipe and the mouthpiece tends to freeze due to the extreme cold. After three hours, the mouth piece on my water bag started freezing up, making it impossible to suck out water. This happened even though I had been blowing water back from the pipe into the water bag in my backpack. To solve the problem, I had to place the mouth piece inside my jacket and against my skin to melt the ice.

After five hours, everyone was getting very tired and it was becoming increasingly apparent that we were all starting to become completely exhausted. The mountain was really wearing down one of my climbing buddies who had fallen prey to a stomach bug. He had begun walking slower and slower, and was having more and more difficulty moving his feet. He looked completely wiped out at this point, and we still had a ways to go. Our guide eventually advised that he descend before he got really ill. One of the guides helped him down to base camp where he waited several hours for us to return We hated to see him leave our group, but he had no choice.

By 3 a.m., many other climbers that we did not know had fallen ill. A bit earlier on our climb, we had to move aside to allow a French family to pass us. We were amazed at how fast they were ascending. Then we came across them sitting on some rocks. Their daughter, who might have been in her early twenties, was crying and vomiting. Clearly they were ascending too fast and she was suffering from acute mountain sickness

(AMS). We also saw a middle-aged gentleman being rushed down by his guides. He could barely walk. They had their arms around his shoulders and practically dragged him towards the descent route. Getting to a lower altitude quickly is the best thing for anyone suffering AMS.

I remember how dark it was throughout the whole climb and that the stars were amazing. They were so bright and vibrant. I never knew how numerous the stars were in the night sky until I saw them from Kilimanjaro. There was no light around to detract from their brilliance. There was nothing to take away from the awe. So we climbed on under the stars, on towards the summit.

Day 5

The group of three in front of us were now about an hour ahead of us. Allen and I kept going one step at a time. By 6:00 a.m. we saw the sun rising, which lightened our hearts a bit especially since we had now being climbing for more than 7 hours. We were struggling as we climbed, and we kept talking to each other, encouraging each other and making sure that we each stayed positive. We were painfully aware of each step as we moved upwards. By 7:30, we reached Stella point. We thought we had reached the top, but alas it was not to be. Our guides told us to take a quick break, but said we should not rest too long and warned us not to lie down or close our eyes. After a few minutes, they encouraged

The ridge on the final stretch to the summit.

us to tackle the last stretch of our climb: the ridge that led to the summit of Kilimanjaro.

It was the hardest part of the climb. We could only take one step at a time, and we continued encouraging each other with each and every one. The trek was made harder because of the slippery volcanic rock powder underfoot. Sometimes we took a few steps up only to slip a step or two back. A climber who was on is way down must have seen the look on my face because he turned around and walked a little of the way with me. He said that it was only another few minutes and that I should not give up. He promised that it was worth it. With that, the stranger left to continue his descent. After this absolutely brutal climb, not one of us was going to be denied reaching the summit.

To this day, I still don't know where the strength came from that got me up that final ridge to the top. There waiting for Allen and me was the other group of three who had been ahead of us. There were tears of joy and relief. The summit was quiet, peaceful and a little eerie. It's a feeling I will never forget.

The view from the top was spectacular.

LIFE'S LESSONS: KEEP YOUR VISION IN MIND

For the most part, it was the vision that got me to the top of Kilimanjaro. I made a promise to myself that I was not going to return from this trek without a piece of lava rock from the top of the summit for each of my sons and for my wife. I had to filter out all the negative messages from my mind that said "Give up. It's enough already." I focused on one step at a time and NEVER lost faith that I would do it.

So many people give up on their dreams because they lose faith or lose focus. I'm not suggesting that you should continue with an idea if the idea turns out to be a lemon. That's foolhardy and could even be dangerous. I'm talking about meeting objectives that are aggressive but realistic. Think about these two examples that demonstrate the power of the mind:

Roger Bannister was the first person ever to run the mile in under four minutes. He did so on May 6, 1954, in a meet at Oxford where he was competing for the British Amateur Athletic Association. At age 25, Roger Bannister had made history. Within a month, the Australian runner John Landy had broken Bannister's record and soon thereafter it was broken many times over.

Sir Edmund Hillary was one of the first climbers to summit Mount Everest. On May 29, 1953, at the age of 33, he and sherpa mountaineer Tenzing Norgay became the first climbers known to have reached the highest point on earth. Since then, more than 4,000 climbers have ascended the mountain.

What do these two men have in common? After they achieved their remarkable feats, thousands of others were inspired to achieve what they had done. Why? I think it was because they knew it was possible, that it could be done. They, like I had done on the upward climb, eradicated any thoughts of "impossible" from their minds and, even more importantly, they never wavered from their vision.

Seven Steps to Help You Achieve Your Objectives

There are libraries of excellent books on the topic of motivation and that share advice on how to deal with challenges. But since I am on the subject, here are seven steps that I believe summarise what many leaders and motivators advocate as key steps to achieving objectives.

1. **Goals.** Most people have goals, and whether the goals focus on finances, personal achievement or just simple day-to-day achievements there are certain basic principles that need be applied when setting them. When I climbed Kilimanjaro, I set some very specific goals, which I organized according to the principle SMART. **SMART** illustrates the five characteristics of an efficient objective: **S**pecific—**M**easurable—**A**ttainable—**R**ealistic—**T**imely.

   a. **Specific:** Goals need to be something specific. Often we set goals that are so vague, it's nearly impossible to judge whether we hit them or not. For example, the statement "I will lose weight" is too vague. How will you know if and when you've reached your goal? To say "I will lose five pounds this month" is more specific. At the end of the month it will be a simple matter of weights and measures: take your measurements and get on the scale. My specific goal was to summit Kilimanjaro. However, it was much easier said than done. To achieve my goal, I had to take heed of the other principles.

   b. **Measurable:** Goals need to be measurable. My goal was to climb Kilimanjaro by March 2010. Had I said I wish to climb Kilimanjaro "some time" in the future, I would have set a goal without a time limit, and this would have meant that I might never have climbed the mountain. Setting an objective without a time parameter is just a dream. If you cannot measure it, you cannot manage it.

c. **Attainable:** Goals need to be reasonable and attainable. If my goal had been to climb to the summit of Mount Everest, I would not have achieved it. In fact, the climb would more than likely have killed me. Don't set yourself up for failure by setting goals that are out of reach.

d. **Realistic**: There is often confusion between "achievable" and "realistic." Was climbing Kilimanjaro an achievable goal? Sure it was. Would it have been realistic to do so within three months of the decision? Probably not. Goals are made achievable when they are set in realistic frameworks. Setting a goal to climb Kilimanjaro within a year of making the decision to do so was an achievable and realistic goal.

e. **Timely**: Goals need to have a time frame. Some people spend a lot of time talking about what they want to do "someday," but without an end date there is no sense of urgency, no reason to take any action today. Having a specific time frame gives you the impetus to get started. It also helps if you monitor your progress. I knew that I had to start training for the climb in a timely manner if I was to be ready for the climb by March 2010.

2. **Attitude.** I have read numerous quotes by famous and successful people, none of which match the one that was quoted to me when we were preparing for the climb. When reviewing the ins-and-outs of altitudes, one of our guides wisely summed it up by saying, "**Altitude is determined by attitude.**" If we had the wrong attitude, we would never have summited Kilimanjaro regardless

of how fit we were. Surround yourself with people who have a positive attitude and draw off their strengths. People with negative attitudes wear you down.

3. **Manage Fear:** I have spoken to many successful people both in business and in the arts, and they all have one thing in common. Can you guess what that is? It's fear. No matter how experienced they are, they know what fear is, and, even more importantly, they've learned how to manage it. If left unmanaged, fear can quickly get in the way of your success. It will prevent you from accomplishing your goals and interfere with your intuition, which is a critical skill for making strong decisions. The more effectively you manage your fear, the sooner you'll accomplish your goals.

   I have experienced fear in many different situations. They range from being fearful of my kids getting hurt, fearful of flying in a really bad storm, fearful of uncertain business deals, fearful that I might get sick and not be able to look after my family. A friend of mine who has a psychology and consultative background once gave me these very good tips.

   a. Know that you have a fear, accept it and don't fight it. Having fear is okay because fear tells us to avoid dangerous situations, puts us on guard and ensures that we move forward with caution.

   b. I know it's not easy but try not to analyse why you are fearful. It's like arguing with a very good lawyer—

Minutes before the commencement of the summit climb. Now this is what you call fear!

you will not win (unless of course you are also a very good lawyer!). Just accept the fact that you have the license to be fearful and that it can work in your favour.

c. Don't allow fear to consume you because rather than working for you it will exacerbate the problem that is causing the fear. Once you have accepted that you are fearful, take some time out and do something enjoyable, like taking a walk, going on a bike ride, working out at the gym—whatever it takes to take your mind off the problem. Having a break will work wonders to help you think more clearly.

d. Get rid of negative noise. I alluded to this just above. People or influences around you that create a negative karma are bad for you. As well, you need to discipline your mind and learn to tune out negative thoughts, the way I did on that final climb to the summit.

e. Seek help. There are lots of resources available that can help you resolve or manage your issue, whatever it might be. There is no reason to take on your burden alone. When we were tackling the summit, we were all feeling anxious and we reduced our fear by talking about it and accepting it. Then we could get on with the task of climbing.

There are several ways to identify FEAR. Here are a few popular acronyms:

- False Evidence Appearing Real.
- False Expectations Appearing Real.
- Face Everything And Recover.
- Forget Everything And Run (polite form).
- Future Events Appearing Real.

- Finding Excuses And Reasons.
- False Expectations About Reality.

4. **Humour.** At the end of the list of things I wanted to take with me on my journey was the word "humour." There were many occasions on the climb that could have triggered negative emotions but which I dispelled with humour. One such occasion comes to mind. When we were on our way up the final stretch of the summit, we saw a young woman vomiting from altitude sickness. Her group was pushing her to keep going. Stupid but true. Given how tired we were and seeing this sight was enough to discourage us. Mario, one of our group yelled out to them, "Where the hell are you going? Are you late for a dental appointment? Slow down, already, you are going to kill this girl." While it might sound corny now, it broke the tension at the time and everyone laughed at his ridiculous rhetorical question. I have been in many business negotiations where tension was broken with some tasteful humour. Never be scared to use it (tastefully), and especially when tension is in the air. Oh, and remember to enjoy the moment.
5. **Staying power.** There is no question in my mind that the last three hours walking to the top of the summit were harder than the first five days of the climb. It would have been so easy to give up, but our determination and commitment kept us going one step at time. I have heard many sad stories of people giving up even though they are so close to achieving their objectives. This is not to say that there are many valid reasons why this might be necessary, such as when my friend became ill and had to turn back. Had he continued to the top, he would have put his life at risk. As close as he was to the top and as determined as he was to reach it, he made the

responsible decision to make the descent. In business, I have often "pulled the plug" on a business idea, making the decision to regard all the time and money spent as sunk. Then again, I have made plenty of mistakes where I moved forward on a losing proposition even when my own instinct told me to stop. Knowing when to stop and cut your losses takes guts.

If you are into long-distance running or have friends who are, then you will relate to this story. For most runners, the last 10 km (6 miles) of a 20-kilometre marathon is the toughest. It means you're almost there: only 10 km to the finish. But it also means the toughest part is yet to come. In fact, many runners consider the marathon to be two races in one: the first 20 miles (42 km) and the last 10 miles (16 km) That's because in the last 10 km, you're exerting the most effort. Your legs are complaining and your mind feels a little cloudy. Some call it "hitting the wall." But with proper training, nutrition and mental strategies, you can make the last 10 km of your marathon. It may be the toughest thing you will ever do, but you will stand a decent chance of getting to the finishing line.

So how does this example relate to business? The first three to five years are the toughest. I have started a few new companies and have experienced the pain of "hanging in" during those early years. As well, I have seen my fair share of small businesses fail just because the owners didn't have the nerve to continue. Operating a small business takes guts and tenacity, and there are thousands of success stories out there. In short—**Never Say Never**.

6. **Put your thoughts into action.** I had to climb the mountain and nobody could have done so for me. Well, I could have said that I "got to the top" and not have

done it. I could have had the porters carry me up. I'm sure if I had paid them enough they would have done it. Humour aside, if you want to get somewhere, you need to put your thoughts into action—BY DOING IT YOURSELF.

7. **Commitment.** Ah, one of my favourites. World class athletes are committed. They rise early in the morning to train, often work at a job during the day only to work out again in the evening. While commitment at this level is extreme, the point is well made. If you want to achieve your goals, you absolutely have to be committed. No one can do it for you—it's up to you. I was a bit of a couch potato and had to make a serious commitment to losing weight and getting into shape. Had I not been dedicated and committed, I would never have achieved my goal and fulfilled my vision.

Summary of Learning Outcomes

1. Keep your vision in mind and don't let anyone tell you that you cannot do it.
2. Stay motivated by reading biographies of people who have achieved great things. They will inspire you.
3. Get rid of the negative noise around you.
4. Set goals by using the SMART principle.
5. Maintain a positive attitude at all times.
6. Manage your fears.
7. Maintain your humour.
8. Stay with it and never give up.

Using This Information to Improve My Life

What do you dream of achieving? Make a list of those things you want to achieve. Use the SMART principle above and start planning how to achieve these dreams. Research how other people might have accomplished what you are seeking to do and start communicating with them through online forums. Your dream might be to summit a mountain or run a marathon. Or maybe you want to be an artist, learn to play a musical instrument, or write a book. There are no limits to translating your dreams into reality.

We have two ears and one mouth so that we can listen twice as much as we speak.
—Epictetus

Six

Communication

The topic of communication is perhaps one of the most discussed topics "out there." It relates to verbal, audio, visual, and body language. There are thousands of books and articles written about the topic, so I will not belabour it for too long. I will relate, however, our experience of how good communication can save lives or how the lack of communication can make a pleasant experience into an unpleasant experience and even a dangerous one.

Prior to the climb, each of us in our group communicated with one another on a regular basis about our training schedules, fitness progress, and what we were taking with us. We communicated with the tour company that booked our flights and organized our climb. We communicated with a doctor who specialised in extreme sports with a special interest in high altitude climbing. He gave us invaluable advice on many do's and don'ts when travelling to eastern Africa, including providing us with the necessary immunization injections necessary for visiting Tanzania. He also prescribed Diamox, a drug that helps reduce altitude sickness. When we arrived in Tanzania, we needed to communicate with the guides about our schedules, and so on. During the ascent and especially on the night of the climb to the summit, the guides continually asked us various questions relating to our health: Are you feeling nauseous? How many fingers on my hand? What is your name? Are you drinking sufficient fluids? These types of questions were important mostly because the guides wanted to ensure that we remained healthy. A sick climber is bad for business and who wants to carry down a 200-pound adult who cannot even stand! HONEST communication was crucial even to the extent that it could mean life or death.

When we saw so many people suffering from altitude sickness or just descending because they "hit a wall," we began to wonder if the guides or the tour company had communicated the right information. Let's use the example of the young lady who was so ill when we were summiting. I don't know this for sure, but there was a decent chance that the guides with her group didn't clearly communicate the dangers of climbing too fast. We also saw an older guy in his fifties being carried down. Did he really understand the enormity of the task ahead? If he had been properly warned, would he have attempted the climb? Perhaps he would never have attempted the climb if he had been told what to expect. I don't know any of this for certain, but what I do know for sure is that many climbers could have avoided such issues if the proper information had been communicated.

Life's Lessons: Communication

There is so much good material on the market that it would be redundant for me to add words of wisdom that are not freely available with the click of a mouse or a quick visit to your library. I will jut share with you what I believe to be key principles that can help you in your personal and business endeavours.

The list of things that we need to communicate on a daily basis can be endless. It is a sad reality that many personal and business relationships fail because of a lack of communication. I have been through my own share of hardships in both personal and business situations that would have been far less stressful had I at the time had the maturity to have an open and honest discussion. Here are some tips that I have found to be extremely useful.

Candour

> *From the day I joined GE to the day I was named CEO, twenty years later, my bosses cautioned me about my candor. I was labeled abrasive and consistently warned my candor would soon get in the way of my career. … and I'm telling you that it was candor that helped make it work. Jack Welch*

Telling the truth right at the beginning will save you major heartache later on. Repeat your insistence for honesty early and often. Imagine if the tour operating company had said that the adventure would be an easy walk and that major preparation was not necessary. The consequences are not necessary to list—they should be a no brainer. Imagine if ego got in the way and we were not honest with the guides or each other regarding the status of our health or abilities.

This principle applies to matters concerning your personal life as well as your business activities. If you are completely candid with people you will find that you will prevent many arguments and disappointments. This principle speaks again to the concept of managing expectations. Ensure that your expectations are honest and open. Why set yourself up to fail? It's only a question of time before it will catch up with you. Here is a good example that demonstrates this point.

As mentioned earlier on, when I first started off in the manufacturing field I was often coerced by my sales people or customers to deliver product by a certain date knowing full well that my production capacity could not produce the product in time. Fearing that I would lose the order if I did not agree to the commitment, I would agree to take it and, of course, call the customer with all sorts of excuses when it was late. It is hard to portray my level of anxiety and stress every time the phone rang and knowing it would be an angry customer on the other end ready to yell at me. I can still feel myself getting anxious just at the thought of those calls that happened more than 30 years ago. I soon learned that it was better to politely refuse an order that had to be fulfilled under impossible conditions and began to offer alternatives instead. For example,

- offering to produce a product I could deliver on time.
- delivering only the amount that could be produced and shipping the balance later on when it was needed.
- offering to source the product elsewhere for the customer, even if for a higher price.

If all options failed, I learned to say no. The result? I kept the goodwill with the customer with no stress and still sold to them again at a later time.

Now that I'm older and (hopefully) wiser, I reinforce the importance of communication with all my staff. Communicate, communicate, communicate—with our internal people (whom I call internal customers) and with external resources such as customers, vendors, and the bank—and do so honestly and openly. Tackle any identifiable problems at the outset.

For example: I have had occasions over the years to ask vendors if they could supply me with urgent products or services. When I was young and naïve, I insisted that they deliver according to my request or forfeit the order knowing full well that they would probably run late. (After all the customer is always right.) The result? I felt disappointed and angry when products were not delivered on time. What would I do today? I would try to find an alternative solution, failing which I would ask the vendor to please be honest with me. If the vendor can't deliver, then I would rather find the product elsewhere and buy from them in the future when I wasn't in such a rush.

I have also learned that being candid with the bank pays good dividends. In my 35 years in business I have never had a bank manager call me to say that I am overdrawn. My late father taught me well. He always made a point of ensuring that he was on top of his financial numbers and called the bank to ask if it was okay to overdraw a certain amount for an exact period of time. Once approved, he ensured that he delivered on his promise no matter how tough it was to find the money to repay the loan. I have lived by this principle all my life and have always been proud of my credit rating as a result.

I have interviewed hundreds if not thousands of job applicants in my business life and I have identified one common mistake that most of them make. They lie. Granted they are not all big lies, but they are lies. In my later years, I have found ways of establishing the truth (no, I don't use a baseball bat). I have been disappointed so often through believing what applicants tell me that, in addition to testing their technical skills, I now look them in the eye and say something like this: "I can teach competence but I cannot teach attitude. I would rather you tell me the whole truth and nothing but the truth so that I can fully evaluate how best to work with you." I also say, "If you oversell yourself by not being candid right now, at the beginning, then it's only a matter of time before the lies will catch up with you."

I could provide you with hundreds of examples that demonstrate this point. However, they all have one thing in common: the importance of being candid. If everyone behaved in such a manner, I guess we would live in a much less stressful world and lawyers would struggle to make a living.

Etiquette

Etiquette is also a form of communication and has a lot to do with good manners. It's not so much our own good manners, but making other people feel comfortable by the way we behave. So it's more or less thinking of others and how others perceive us, so that everyone knows the rules for doing things and everyone is in a very comfortable position in society.

Etiquette describes the conventional requirements of social behaviour and the proprieties of conduct for each class, community or occasion. What is considered good etiquette in one culture may be offensive in another. For example, in some countries it is acceptable to eat with ones hands whereas in other cultures it is not regarded as good etiquette.

Good manners display respect, care and consideration for others. Good manners can help you to have better relationships with people you know and those you will meet.

Good and bad manners are also a form of communication. It tells someone what a person is made of. It communicates a message about how they think and behave and is one of the silent languages like body language which I will get to later.

Here are some simple examples of every day bad manners that make me crazy:

- People not saying "thank you" when someone has done them a favour or has been nice.
- Employees not saying good morning or goodbye when they arrive at or leave the office.
- Suppliers or customers not returning phone messages.

The list is endless. These small things count. These are things by which others will judge you. Here are some simple tips on how manners can be improved and how they will help you in society, job seeking and friendships. These rules apply to anyone regardless of age and status.

Language

I completed my military training, so believe me when I tell you that there are very few swear words that I do not know. I am sure that you, the reader of this book, have probably heard unnecessary profanity as well. It only cheapens your opinion of the people who speak this way. It goes without saying that most of us will use profanity from time to time, especially when under pressure. There may be a time and place for the use of inappropriate language, given the circumstances and audience, but crude jokes and foul language can be offensive to some people. This applies especially when in the company of customers or suppliers. It is simply unprofessional. It crosses the line from professional to personal and could be very costly if a customer leaves you because you offended them.

People will judge you based on appearances

Pay attention to how you carry yourself. Don't slouch. Maintain a neat appearance. Shake hands firmly. Employ proper hygiene. Hold your head high. Don't wear sunglasses indoors or wear other "trying to be cool" looks at the wrong time: it gives the impression of arrogance and immaturity. Arriving at an interview for a job, or to sell your products or services, with unpolished shoes, dirty clothing or a dishevelled look will not impress anyone. People assume that a person's inattention to these details will translate into a similar approach to doing business. This even applies when the job is in a casual environment. Looking after yourself means you respect yourself, which translates into "I have respect for you and your company". It makes the statement, "I care".

Phone etiquette

How many times have you seen people on their cell phones or attending to e-mails at the dinner table or while in a meeting? Because it's a common practice doesn't mean it's not rude.

Unless there is an absolute emergency, there is no reason to have to take or make phone calls when in the presence of others.

Communication with work colleagues

I am an avid reader and enjoy heeding the wisdom of gifted authors. Stephen Covey who wrote the popular *7 Habits of Highly Successful People*, wrote the following article in his book *The 8th Habit*.

He describes a poll of 23,000 employees drawn from a number of companies and industries. He reports the poll's findings:

- Only 37 percent said they have a clear understanding of what their organization is trying to achieve and why.
- Only one in five was enthusiastic about their team's and their organization's goals.
- Only one in five said they had a clear "line of sight" between their tasks and their team's and organization's goals.
- Only 15 percent felt that their organization fully enables them to execute key goals.
- Only 20 percent fully trusted the organization they work for.

Then, Covey superimposes a very human metaphor over the statistics. He says, "If, say, a soccer team had these same scores, only 4 of the 11 players on the field would know which goal is theirs. Only 2 of the 11 would care. Only 2 of the 11 would know what position they play and know exactly what they are supposed to do. And all but 2 players would, in some way, be competing against their own team members rather than the opponent."

Communicating and understanding

In 1990, Elizabeth Newton earned a Ph.D. in psychology at Stanford by studying a simple game in which she assigned people to one of two roles: "tappers" or "listeners." Tappers received a list of twenty-five well-known songs, such as "Happy Birthday to You" and "The Star Spangled Banner." Each tapper was asked to pick a song and tap out the rhythm to a listener (by knocking on a table). The listener's job was to guess the song, based on the rhythm being tapped.

The listener's job in this game was quite difficult. Over the course of Newton's experiment, 120 songs were tapped out. Listeners guessed only 2.5 percent of the songs: 3 out of 120. But here's what made the result worthy of a dissertation in psychology. Before the listeners guessed the name of the song, Newton asked the tappers to predict the odds that the listeners would guess correctly. They predicted that the odds would be 50 percent. The tappers actually succeeded only 1 time in 40, but they thought they were getting their message across 1 out of every 2 times. Why? When a tapper tapped, she heard the song in her head. It was impossible to avoid hearing the tune internally. Meanwhile, the listeners couldn't hear that tune—all they could hear were a bunch of disconnected taps, like a bizarre Morse Code.

It was hard to be a tapper. The problem was that tappers (teachers) have been given knowledge (the song title) that made it impossible for them to imagine what it was like to lack that knowledge. When they tapped, they couldn't imagine what it was like for the listeners (the student) to hear isolated taps rather than a song.

This is called the Curse of Knowledge. Once we know something, we find it hard to imagine what it was like not to know it. And it becomes difficult for us to share our knowledge with others, because we can't readily re-create our listeners' state of mind.

The point is this: never assume that the person with whom you are communicating fully understands what you are trying to convey. When we were on the mountain, the guides didn't just ask if we were OK (it's one of the things they did right). They asked us questions such as "How many fingers am I holding up?" or "What is your friends name that is standing next you?" While these simple questions were just testing our level of lucidity, the principle demonstrates the importance of verifying the transfer of information.

Creating your personal brand: it's all about how you communicate and how you are perceived

People who want to become business leaders understand that they themselves are a product brand. They are authentic, dependable and reliable. Their icon is their name. Delivering the best of themselves is their brand promise. Do you want to become a winner at working? Then, deliver the brand promise.

Brand promise is what you say to the customer and what you deliver. If you are not able to meet the expectations of the customer, your business will either flounder or die. If you are not able to deliver the brand promise you will not be able to meet the expectations that have been created in the customer's mind.

Tom Peters is a world renowned business guru who has transformed many businesses. He is the author of many books, but none more famous than *In Search of Excellence*. Peters is credited with saying "Formula for success: under promise and over deliver".

It can take years to build a good reputation, but only take one bad decision to destroy it.

You are always on trial. The customer, whether it be your boss, colleague, friend or any other associate, is the judge, juror, and executor.

Personal branding

Dorothy Lazovik is a premier personal brand strategist who advises individuals from all walks of life. Here are some highlights from her teachings to help you impact your brand and stand out for who you are.

You have a choice in everything you communicate, verbally and non-verbally, to influence how people perceive you. This perception can be formed in person, through observation, by word of mouth or virtually that dictates your personal brand.

In simple terms your personal brand becomes what others are saying about you when you are not there.

The good news is that you have absolute control over what you reveal about yourself to others. The message you deliver needs to differentiate you from everyone else. In other words how can you can stand out and get heard above the noise? Essentially, your personal brand is what can set you apart from your competition.

Apple positioned their difference and at the time of writing has become the most valuable company in the world. Starbucks went against the belief that no one would pay four dollars for a cup of coffee and now is a multi billion dollar international company. Oprah decided to follow her heart and that lead to having the largest viewing audience in the world. Richard Branson (Founder of Virgin) pushed the boundaries of what was possible and grew an international brand that has created a multi billion dollar empire. Not bad for a high school drop out!

Whether we are referring to products or people, the steps and rules are the same. Successful brands have a clear and well defined message. They know who they are and how they want to be known. They are not afraid to be different and don't expect to be liked by everyone. You as an individual are no different.

"The easiest way to create success is to be yourself. No one plays that role better than you!"

Come to terms with who you are so that you can be the best at who you are rather than turning yourself into someone you are not. Why? Because it's far easier to be authentic than attempting to manage the stress of acting like someone you're not.

To build a personal brand that supports who you are, here are the five key principles that can have an immediate positive impact on your life.

1. Plan your success by managing perceptions.

Focus on the impression you want to create about yourself while remembering that first impressions are lasting impressions. Even though a first impression is only a snapshot of who you really are, first impressions serve as a filter for all future interactions. You have lots of opportunities to practice this concept every day. The key is to know the impression you want to create ahead of time.

Visualize walking into a social event that presents the opportunity for you to speak with some high profile people that you admire. When you walk away from that conversation what are the words you would love to hear them use to describe who you are? What is the impression that you want to leave behind?

Give serious consideration to the words you want to own in the minds of others and how you want them to see you. These words become your guideline for how you behave, what you say, how you say it and what you wear to create the perception you intend.

Ensure that all communications from you and about you are consistent with the image and perception you want to create about yourself.

2. Know who you really are.

At your core you are a combination of your unique attitudes, natural talents, strengths, passions, values and beliefs. These are the intangible elements that others don't always see.

These intangible elements are the internal operating system that drives your decisions and behaviors. They are revealed in your actions, your words and how you present yourself. When you learn to be conscious of them, they make your life so much easier!

Give thought to the behaviours you need to demonstrate, or the activities you need to engage in, that support your core values, natural talents, key strengths and passions. Make them obvious, both professionally and personally, to other people!

Keep in mind that no person or circumstance can force you to conduct yourself in a manner you cannot control.

Neville and his group were clearly exhausted and probably felt somewhat inconvenienced at times. Don't you think that any one of them were tempted to lash out because they were tired and hurting? More than once would be my guess but they chose not to. Why? Because they had a common goal and they all knew that lashing out wouldn't get them what they all ultimately wanted and nor would it have served the group or themselves in a positive way.

When you feel grounded in who you are, it allows you to deal calmly with a situation you are facing and not get emotionally engaged in the conflict or chaos. It eliminates the second-guessing and provides the opening to just resolve the situation at hand.

Responding to a situation instead of reacting is powerful. This is a great way to stand out and thrive!

3. Position your difference.

You do this by identifying the one key strength you want to be known for. Most people are typically good at more than one thing but will excel at what comes naturally to them. For example: if you have a talent for creating computer games, you spend endless hours doing so and love it! In other words when using this strength you always feel like you have energy to spare. In fact this is true for most hobbies.

Word of Caution: You may take this skill for granted because it comes so easy to you. You might even find yourself saying, "Oh anybody can do that!" That is simply not true and no one can do it like you!

Your difference is the magic ingredient that separates you from everyone else. It is that special "something" only you can do. It is not just what you do that creates the magic, it is how you do it that sets you apart from the crowd. Using the gaming example, identify the type of gamer that makes your work special and keep tweaking it to improve upon the skill.

One way to discover the magic ingredient is to listen to feedback from people that you trust.

4. Connect to make a difference.

Communicate in a way that your audience understands.

For example: One of my sisters is a nurse. She shares stories about work that include medical terms and abbreviations I am not familiar with. She uses them so naturally I feel as if I should know them. Being my sister I don't hesitate to say, "Hey what does that mean?" To be understood it is important to use language that your audience can relate to.

Seek first to understand, then to be understood—Stephen Covey (The 7 Habits of Highly Effective People)

If your goal is to influence others to make a decision in your favour, it is critical you first understand them. If you want to discuss a grade with your professor, or a promotion with your boss (who is always a bit crabby before lunch), does it make sense to schedule the meeting right before lunch?

Know your audience and adjust your communication style to make a connection. For example, you will speak differently to a young child versus an adult. You will choose different words when communicating with someone whose command of the English language is limited.

Whether you are talking with a client, friend or family member, or you have an audience of team mates or peers, communicate to connect. Be present by giving your full attention.

"Be more interested in what your audience wants versus what you can get from them."

5. *Consistency is key in everything you do.*

A good franchise is about a consistent predictable experience.

Your personal brand is no different. If you are friendly and helpful one day then short tempered and moody the next, you are being inconsistent and it leaves people wondering what they can expect next.

WARNING! When you start integrating new behaviors to present a stronger brand image it is very easy to slip back to old habits and patterns. Expect to experience setbacks. This way they won't surprise you or take you out of the game. Old habits are elastic and will attempt to pull you back to what you have always done. Catch yourself and reset! Don't stop and don't give up!

The importance of being consistent is that it builds trust and positive brand equity. Positive brand equity is built by repeating behaviors and creating experiences that support your brand (the person you want to be).

Building your brand equity is like building equity in your bank account. To build equity in your bank account you deposit money and watch it grow. To build your personal brand equity you deposit positive consistent behaviors, acts of consideration, active listening, timely follow up, a polished professional image, meeting deadlines, high energy, a positive attitude...EVERY TIME!

Consistency reinforces your brand and allows your audience to know beyond a doubt, exactly what they can expect. Think about well known brands you are familiar with and those I mentioned earlier on: McDonalds, Coke Cola, Apple, Starbucks, etc. Their products or services are all consistent and predictable. Your personal brand should operate on the same principles. Be consistent and predicable and ensure that all your acts and thoughts mirror who you want to be.

I have a close friend and mentor, Brahm, who is unlike most people that I know. In all the years that I have known him, I have never heard him say a bad word about anyone. He is super successful. An amazing family man and a well respected lawyer, he is also friendly, honest, caring and efficient. Whatever Brahm promises, he delivers. Always. He has created a superb personal brand.

It proves to me that one does not have to ridicule others to be successful and happy. There are many people who feel that by denigrating others, they will appear to look better in comparison. Actually, it makes people feel uncomfortable to hear negative comments about others and often makes peers feel less respect for one rather than the positive outcome that they had hoped for.

Summary of learning outcomes

1. Be candid. Telling the truth and communicating reasonable expectations at the front end will save you from either having to make apologetic excuses or having to flog yourself and your staff unmercifully when the deadline comes and it's time to deliver on your promise.
2. Be conscious of your etiquette.
3. Good manners and kindness indicate a person's character.
4. Watch your language. Foul language is offensive to many people.
5. Keep your body healthy. How you look affects others' perceptions of you.
6. Verify that your communication is understood.
7. Follow the 5 rules to build your personal brand.
    a. manage perceptions.
    b. know who you really are.
    c. differentiate yourself from others.
    d. connect to make a difference.
    e. be consistent in everything that you do.

Using this information to improve my life

1. List all those times that you think you may have messed up due to miscommunication. List how you might have said things differently.
2. List what you should do to change the way you look so that you can portray a better image of yourself.
3. Make a list of those habits that interfere with your branding and commit to stopping them (e.g., bad language, using your phone when at the dinner table with friends or business colleagues).

I can accept failure, everyone fails at something. But I can’t accept not trying.
—Michael Jordan

Seven

It's Tough on the Way Down

The descent was brutally steep.

As we stood at the top of Kilimanjaro, the highest free standing mountain in the world, the peace, serenity and awe mesmerized us. It was unfortunate that were only allowed an hour before we began our descent. It was not only very cold but the air was thin and it was tough to breathe. Even though I was not hungry, I knew that it was really important to stay hydrated with adequate nutrition, so I reluctantly ate some trail mix and had some water. After ensuring that I had the volcanic rocks that I promised my wife and children, I hoisted my day pack back on, and started the descent. A friend who had completed the climb a couple of years back gave me a wonderful tip. He advised me to tie the front of my boots really tight. He failed to take heed to this tip and lost his toe nails due to the friction. It was hard for me to believe that the descent could possibly be that steep. We used a different route coming down. It was brutally steep and required great skill not to fall. Imagine descending on sand or snow at a 45 degree angle. The angles were so steep that, without the use of poles, it was tough to even stand still without falling over. We were subjected to every type of terrain imaginable. It started as scree which is very slippery powdered volcanic rock. As we descended we were faced with steep rocks which had to be navigated carefully since our legs were like rubber after the climb. It's really hard on the upper thighs and we had to stop from time to time to wait for the burning sensation to subside. At times the gradient was so steep that we were "surfing" down using the sides of the soles of our boots which acted like mini skis. We all had our turns at falling and thank goodness none of us were hurt. I heard of a story recently about a very fit man in his 30's who slipped and had a really bad fall. He broke his arm and was badly concussed. He was carried down by the guides and when they got to one of the camps that was low enough he was airlifted by helicopter to a hospital. Yes, it's that dangerous.

As I recall it took about 4 hours to reach Barafu camp which is the base camp where we stayed the night before the summit. The porters were there waiting for us to provide us with much needed fluid and nutrition. We were all on the verge of tears from exhaustion. I will remind you that we left this camp at 11:00 pm the night before, climbed all night to reach the summit at 8:30 the next morning and arrived back at the camp at about 2:00pm the next day. Remember that we had no sleep and burned more than 6,000 calories. However, our rest was brief. There were no supplies at this barren camp and we had to continue for another 5 hours to the next camp where we would spend the night before the final descent back to the base. My memory is somewhat vague because of a combination of the altitude and exhaustion, but I do recall that this final 5 hours of descent seemed longer that the 6 days it took to get to the top.

By the time we arrived at the next and final camp I felt broken in every way. I felt spiritually spent and every part of my body hurt. I slept like a baby that night despite the extreme discomfort of the tent being on a rocky surface. I just didn't care. Sleep, blissful sleep.

The next morning I awoke to the sound of chirping birds, the aroma of freshly brewed coffee and lots of groaning coming from the tents of my climbing pals. There wasn't a muscle in my body that didn't ache but the journey was not yet over.

Although the gradient had significantly decreased it was still about a 12 km (8 miles) trek to the end. The ground was muddy and uneven and very hard to navigate, so it was easy to lose one's footing and fall. My legs felt like rubber. We arrived back at the base of the mountain in the early afternoon and headed back to the hotel in the Land Rover.

The hotel room and facilities were a welcome sight.

Life's Lesson

No matter who you are, every person will have obstacles, setbacks, and outright failures.

Many entrepreneurs have their business heroes. Some are revered not only for their huge successes but for the setbacks they endured and subsequently overcame. In other words they had their share of successes but had to manage themselves when they "went down" so to speak . We experienced how tough it was coming down the mountain. Although this was a physical experience that ended with a positive outcome, metaphorically the principle was not very different from the ups and downs we experience in our personal and business lives. It's largely a question of attitude and how we deal with life's obstacles. Recognizing that everyone has obstacles helps too.

Rather than share my own views on the power of attitude when "the chips are down" I'm going to share some inspiring stories and quotes of famous people who never allowed failures to get the better of them. It's always easy to blame others and circumstances when we fail. We should, however, take a look in the mirror and say "I have a choice. I can either sulk and blame everyone but myself or I can pick myself up and dust myself off and find ways to work harder, be smarter and learn from my mistakes". I hope you are as inspired as I am when reading these stories.

Did you know that:

Winston Churchill failed sixth grade. He was subsequently defeated in every election for public office until he became Prime Minister at the age of 62. He later wrote, "Never give in, never give in, never, never, never, never-in nothing, great or small, large or petty-never give in except to convictions of honor and good sense. Never, Never, Never, Never give up."

Sigmund Freud was booed from the podium when he first presented his ideas to the scientific community of Europe. He returned to his office and kept on writing.

Thomas Edison's teachers said he was "too stupid to learn anything." He was fired from his first two jobs for being "non-productive".

Albert Einstein did not speak until he was 4-years-old and did not read until he was 7. His parents thought he was "sub-normal," and one of his teachers described him as "mentally slow, unsociable, and adrift forever in foolish dreams." He was expelled from school and was refused admittance to the Zurich

Polytechnic School. He did eventually learn to speak and read. Even to do a little math.

Louis Pasteur was only a mediocre pupil in undergraduate studies and ranked 15th out of 22 students in chemistry.

Henry Ford failed and went broke five times before he succeeded.

R. H. Macy failed seven times before his store in New York City caught on.

When Bell telephone was struggling to get started, its owners offered all their rights to Western Union for $100,000. The offer was disdainfully rejected with the pronouncement, "What use could this company make of an electrical toy."

An expert said of **Vince Lombardi**: "He possesses minimal football knowledge and lacks motivation." Lombardi would later write, "It's not whether you get knocked down; it's whether you get back up."

Michael Jordan and Bob Cousy were each cut from their high school basketball teams. Jordan once observed, "I've failed over and over again in my life. That is why I succeed."

Stan Smith was rejected as a ball boy for a Davis Cup tennis match because he was "too awkward and clumsy." He went on to clumsily win Wimbledon and the U. S. Open. And eight Davis Cups.

Walt Disney was fired by a newspaper editor because "he lacked imagination and had no good ideas." He went bankrupt several times before he built Disneyland. In fact, the proposed park was rejected by the city of Anaheim on the grounds that it would only attract riffraff.

Charles Schultz had every cartoon he submitted rejected by his high school yearbook staff. Oh, and Walt Disney wouldn't hire him.

After his first audition, **Sidney Poitier** was told by the casting director, "Why don't you stop wasting people's time and go out and become a dishwasher or something?" It was at that moment, recalls Poitier, that he decided to devote his life to acting.

The first time **Jerry Seinfeld** walked on-stage at a comedy club as a professional comic, he looked out at the audience, froze, and forgot the English language. He stumbled through "a minute-and a half" of material and was jeered offstage. He returned the following night and closed his set to wild applause.

After **Harrison Ford's** first performance as a hotel bellhop in the film Dead Heat on a Merry-Go-Round, the studio vice-president called him in to his office. "Sit down kid," the studio head said, "I want to tell you a story. The first time Tony Curtis was ever in a movie he delivered a bag of groceries. We took one look at him and knew he was a movie star." Ford replied, "I thought you were supposed to think that he was a grocery delivery boy." The vice president dismissed Ford with "You ain't got it kid , you ain't got it ... now get out of here."

Michael Caine's headmaster told him, "You will be a laborer all your life."

When **Pablo Casals** reached 95, a young reporter asked him "Mr. Casals, you are 95 and the greatest cellist that ever lived. Why do you still practice six hours a day?" Mr. Casals answered, "Because I think I'm making progress."

English crime novelist **John Creasey** got 753 rejection slips before he published 564 books.

Here are some inspiring examples of famous businesses that had to manage on their way down before becoming successful again.

Company: The Body Shop

When Roddick opened the first Body Shop, a beauty products company, in Brighton, U.K., in 1976, two neighboring funeral parlors initially objected to the name. Roddick fought back by suggesting to a local newspaper that she was a woman entrepreneur under siege. The publicity generated traffic to the store, and by the early 1990s, there were more than 700 Body Shop stores.

Lesson: Don't let minor setbacks throw you off course.

Company: Federal Express (now FedEx Corp.)

After revolutionizing overnight mail delivery in the 1970s, Smith introduced an electronic delivery service, Zapmail, in 1984 to compete with fax machines. But Zapmail didn't draw the anticipated interest and cost the company nearly $350 million over two years. FedEx abandoned Zapmail in 1986 and the company refocused its energy on its core delivery business. The company generated $35 billion in revenue in 2010.
Lesson: Be willing to acknowledge failure, abandon bad ideas and move on

Company: The Walt Disney Co. (now Disney Corp.)

The cartoon animation pioneer weathered several major financial setbacks in the late 1920s and 1930s, including losing rights to the popular Oswald the Lucky Rabbit character. His company was $4 million in debt by the early 1930s. With barely enough cash to finance the project, Disney released "Snow White and the Seven Dwarfs" in 1938. The blockbuster movie sprung the company out of bankruptcy and bankrolled the building of a new Walt Disney Studios in Burbank, Calif.
Lesson: One killer idea can quickly make up for a series of flops.

Company: Apple Computer

After his forced resignation from Apple in 1985, Jobs spent the following several years developing NeXT, a computer workstation for educators. But with a high price tag and reports of numerous bugs, sales never materialized. The company burned through hundreds of millions of investor dollars. Apple announced it would buy NeXT in 1996, bringing Jobs back to the company as interim CEO. He's since developed the iPod

and iPad, making Apple one of the most successful Fortune 500 companies of the past decade.
Lesson: Having the right resources and people around you makes a big difference.

Company: Wendy's

Thomas retired as Wendy's CEO in 1982, 13 years after founding what had become one of the largest fast-food chains in the U.S. Within years, the company revenues sagged as some customers were unimpressed with a new breakfast menu, and cleanliness and service standards slipped at franchises. One of the company's leading franchisees, James Near, became its top executive and managed a turnaround. Thomas came out of semi-retirement and filled a crucial role as the company's spokesman in its advertisements, leading one of the company's most-successful advertising campaigns.
Lesson: Having a strong leader at the helm can make a world of difference in the success or failure of a company.

Martha Stewart

Martha Stewart successfully built her company "Martha Stewart Living OmniMedia" from scratch and became a billionaire. But she made a mistake (insider trading) that negatively affected her reputation and landed her in jail. Being an entrepreneur with guts; she refused to be cowed by her mistakes and she bounced back to fortune and fame. This is what she has to say about her mistake and resulting failure.

"I know I have a very tough five months ahead of me, but I understand, too, that I will get through those months knowing that I have the ability to return to my productive and normal life, my interesting work and future business opportunities." —Martha Stewart.

"My new motto is: When you're through changing, you're through."—Martha Stewart

Donald Trump

Donald Trump is a savvy real estate billionaire that has gone through bankruptcy on two separate occasions. He once had a personal debt of $1billion and corporate debt of $9billion but he pulled himself out of the mess and this is what he has to say about his business failures.

"Anyone who thinks my story is anywhere near over is sadly mistaken."

"Sometimes by losing a battle, you will find a new way to win the war."

"I was relentless even in the face of total lack of encouragement because much more often than you think; sheer persistence is the difference between success and failure."

There are lots more stories such as these and every time I feel uninspired or despondent I read these types of stories which gives me encouragement. I have had my share of ups and downs in both my personal and business life and I bounce back up again when latching onto the courage of others who know how to navigate themselves down so that they can manage their way up again.

Is it easy? Of course not. So how did these people do it? Hard work and determination. Plain and simple. Don't assume that anything will get handed to you or that someone had it handed to them. If you have dreams, goals and success that you want in your life then buckle down, plan it out and work your tail off trying to make it happen. Don't ever wait for success to find you. If you do, you'll be standing there for quite some time all alone.

I believe that there is one thing that all successful people practice and it can be summarised in three words: **Focus focus focus.**

It doesn't matter what your project might be. If its studying, then focus on your studies. If it's a job, focus on doing it better. If is about struggling with a personal relationship then focus or resolving your issues. If you're in business, focus on your core skills and keep trying to improve them. Earlier on I alluded to the importance of patience; so many people expect things to happen “now” with an attitude of entitlement. Perfection takes time. Whether it’s to learn a subject at school or skill at work. It all takes time.

The 10,000 hour rule: Source Wikipedia

Outliers: The Story of Success is a non-fiction book written by Malcolm Gladwell who examines the factors that contribute to high levels of success. To support his thesis, he examines the causes of why the majority of Canadian ice hockey players are born in the first few months of the calendar year, how Microsoft co-founder Bill Gates achieved his extreme wealth, how The Beatles became one of the most successful musical acts in human history, how cultural differences play a large part in perceived intelligence and rational decision making, and how two people with exceptional intelligence, Christopher Langan and J. Robert Oppenheimer, end up with such vastly different fortunes. Throughout the publication, Gladwell repeatedly mentions the “10,000-Hour Rule”, claiming that the key to success in any field is, to a large extent, a matter of practicing a specific task for a total of around 10,000 hours. How long is that:

If you work 8 hours a day for 5 days a week it will take you almost 5 years to work 10,000 hours.

I’m not suggesting that we are all made of the stuff that will make us famous or turn us into millionaires. I have worked hard all my life. I understand that it takes hard work to get somewhere. However I was not always the most tidy or well organised guy around and I had to learn how to manage myself so that I didn’t spend my days dreaming away. I guess I had a bit of ADD when I was growing up and had to learn to manage it. This brings us to the next chapter about getting organised and staying focused.

> *Nothing can stop the man with right mental attitude from achieving his goal; nothing on earth can help the man with the wrong mental attitude.*
>
> **—Thomas Jefferson**

Summary of learning outcomes

1. Every successful person has had failures.
2. When a project does not work, manage the process "on the way down."
3. Learn from your mistakes.
4. Never, never, never give up.
5. It takes 10,000 hours to perfect a skill.

Using this information to improve my life:

1. List the occasions where you have, in your opinion, failed. Then list the mistakes that led to the failures and what you could have done to avoid them.
2. List those projects that have not worked and identify those that in your opinion can still work.
3. Use the SMART principle in chapter 5 and analyse those projects that still have potential and see if they can still work if done differently.
4. Pursue your dreams.

___

___

___

___

___

___

___

Enthusiasm is not the same as just being excited. One gets excited about going on a roller coaster. One becomes enthusiastic about creating and building a roller coaster.

—Bo Bennett

Eight

Maintaining Enthusiasm

It was a huge "come down" after returning home. I had worked for so long and so hard to prepare for the journey and felt quite "deflated" after returning. I really struggled to get back to the gym, stay focused at work and generally get back to my usual level of enthusiasm. Having spoken to friends who are tri-athletes and extreme sports enthusiasts, I have been told that this is a common phenomena and is largely due to a form of burnout. Having researched this issue, I found various ways to get back on track. Given that I am also a person who gets easily distracted, I used the opportunity to sharpen my skills relating to time management and re-energized myself at the same time.

I think this principle is true for most people in many circumstances. Take for example studying for a huge exam or spending days, nights and weekends on a work project. It's really tough to get up and go again after experiencing some burnout. Here is how I manage myself after such experiences and especially after struggling to get back to routine after the climb.

1. **If you cannot measure it you cannot manage it.** Since the only absolute finite resource we have available is time it's important to measure how we are using it and

wasting it. Use a device to record your daily activities that is constantly accessible to you, so you can record exactly what you do when you do it. A Day-Timer or calendar, an organizer application on your computer or smartphone, a digital recorder, or an ordinary notebook will all work for activity tracking; choose whichever method you are comfortable with and find the easiest to use. Don't record unnecessary information; it's the activity and the time you spent on it that's important for our purposes.

2. **Find out where you're wasting time.** Are you spending too much time web surfing, e-mailing, texting etc. Limit the amount of time you spend on mundane unproductive activities. They really do eat away at your valuable time.
3. **Block out time and set goals.** Once you have identified these unproductive activities, set aside your relaxation time to complete these tasks. For example: don't look at e-mails/text messages or surf the net while doing a project. If you have problems concentrating for more than an hour then use blocks of one hour at a time on your projects. Take a short break and go for it again. Ensure that you use your "best hours" to do the hardest projects. For example, I'm a morning guy and pretty brainless in the late afternoons. I therefore make sure that I use my mornings being my best production time to tackle the hardest projects and leave my e-mails etc. to late afternoon. Granted I do look at my inbox to ensure that there is nothing urgent but I have now disciplined myself not to attend to anything that can wait.
4. **Track your progress.** Objectives must be measurable in time and value. For example: if you want to save for a new laptop you will need to know how much needs to be saved by a specific date. There is no point in saying I

want to save $800 to buy it "sometime". Sometime could be any date in the future. Conversely there is little point in saying you want to buy a laptop at the end of March but you have no clue how much you need to save. The two conditions work hand in hand. If you are tracking a project such as an online course, it's important to block out chunks of time to ensure that you don't end up cramming the course in the last minute.

5. **Prioritize.** Start each day with a priority list of what absolutely needs to be completed that day. It's important however to be ruthlessly realistic. If you are too ambitious you will not achieve your goals in the time you set aside which will end in disappointment. For example, when I wrote this book (which is about 30,000 words), I made sure that I set an objective of no less than 1,000 words per session on those days that I set aside to write. That's about four pages of text. I also set a target end date to be ready for editing. Having done that I worked backward from the end date and ensured that the book got done in time.
6. **Establish routines.** Humans are creatures of habit. So if you set yourself some routines, especially during your workweek, you will find yourself getting into a rhythm and it will easier to set aside blocks of time. This works mostly because you can anticipate how you spend your time.
7. **Using unproductive time productively.** There is little that frustrates me more than waiting in line ups, sitting in traffic or waiting for long periods of time waiting for an appointment. I make a point of always taking a book with me or I use the time to attend to e-mails on my iPhone. There is plenty of technology available that allows us to stay connected and to use time productively rather than just twiddling your thumbs. Be prepared.

8. **Use your skills where they yield the best return on your (time) investment.** For example, if you are in the business of computer servicing, are you better off spending time writing invoices and doing your own bookkeeping or is it better to be working on the job generating revenue? Clearly it's better to pay for a bookkeeper so that it relieves you of the burden of doing mundane work and spending your time where its best suited. The message here is "delegate" so that you can free up the time for which you are best suited.
9. **Do what you love to do** and you won't even know where the time went. If you are a student there will be lots of subjects or topics that bore you to death. There will always be times when you have to perform mundane or unpleasant tasks. Do these first thing in the morning and get them out of the way. There are lots of tasks that I really don't like doing such as making calls to customers who are slow paying their bills. I do these chores first thing in the morning to get them out of the way so I can enjoy the rest of the day doing things that I enjoy.
10. **Leave time in your schedule for regular exercise.** Exercise has been touted to do everything from treat depression to improve memory, with the power to cure a host of problems while preventing even more. In particular, exercise leads to the release of certain neurotransmitters in the brain that alleviate pain, both physical and mental. Additionally, it is one of the few ways scientists have found to generate new neurons. Much of the research done in this area has focused on running, but all types of aerobic exercise provide benefits. Although the exact nature of these benefits is still being determined, enough research has been done to provide even sceptics with a motivation to take up

exercise. Oh, and by the way, it's also excellent for our self esteem when we look good!

There are no rules. Do what suits your personality and accept the fact that your priorities will change over time. For example I used to go to the gym early in the mornings. I now prefer to get to the office really early and work out on my way home. In other words I do cerebral work at the time when my brain is functioning at its best. By 5:00 pm I'm no good to anyone, least of all myself, so I leave the office and exercise on my way home.

Get a hobby

Whether your hobby be a sporting activity such as cycling or basketball, or whether it be of a cerebral nature such as chess, it's important to have an outlet outside of work or school. It stimulates the mind, expands your social circle and helps keep life in the balance. You will also be surprised how many people create a new career through their hobbies. What a wonderful way to earn a living doing what you love.

Celebrate success

I know that I'm really hard on myself and sometimes get quite depressed when I don't achieve what I think is expected of me. However I have learned over the years to lighten up a bit and celebrate small successes as they are achieved. I don't mean having a raving party. I mean "I pat myself on my back" and say "good job". I sometimes take my family out for a nice dinner if I made a good sale or finished a new project. I might even take the afternoon off as my reward. It doesn't matter how you celebrate. What's important is that you recognise small and large wins alike and recognize these achievements.

*There are no secrets to success.
It is the result of preparation,
hard work and learning
from failure.
—Colin Powell*

Nine

Conclusion

The goal of this book is to inspire you to strive for more. It is intended to create some stimulating thoughts and methods to help you reach your goals and aspirations. To that end there are a few other inspiring thoughts that I want to share with you, but could not find a placeholder for them in previous chapters. I have therefore assembled them in this chapter.

We cannot always have what we want

Life is not always a bed of roses. Have you ever slept on a hard surface with a rock under your ass? Try it sometime and you will know the true meaning of uncomfortable. Sometimes the conditions are not ideal but we had to live with it and accept it. Would we have preferred a room at the Four Seasons rather than a tent in sub zero temperatures? Of course. Do you think that better golf clubs will help you play better? Perhaps, but if you cannot afford them then make the best of what you've got. There is a big difference between wants and needs. I want a larger TV but do I really need it?

Be grateful

So many people are not grateful for things that they have and take for granted. Here is a simple example to illustrate this point. Imagine that you lost your right thumb in an accident and are right-handed. The impact of the loss of just one finger will be enormous. You will struggle to write, pick things up, zip up your jacket etc. I'm not suggesting that you should spend your day being grateful that you have a thumb but the point is made. Having an education, a job, opportunities that our society offers us, and even just our health, are all points for which we should be grateful. So many people spend their time complaining about what they don't have. I think Oprah says it all with this quote.

Be thankful for what you have and you will end up having more. But if you concentrate on what you don't have, you'll never, ever have enough—Oprah Winfrey

Trust your instincts

Intuition is always right in at least two important ways. It is always in response to something. It always has your best interest at heart.

Sometimes the facts will tell you one thing but your instinct tells you something else.

It is dark and you are walking toward your car in a parking lot. There is a man standing a little away from your car leaning against a pole upon which there is a dim light glowing. You can see his face quite clearly but while he is dressed nicely there is something about his demeanour which scares you. You walk faster and faster toward your car. As you get near your car he starts walking towards you. You quickly fish out your keys unlock the door and get in. You waste no time starting the car and racing off. There was something about him that scared you.

The next morning you read an article in the newspaper that spoke about someone fitting the description of the man you saw being wanted for murder charges and was armed and dangerous. There were no facts to support your feelings but you acted on your instincts.

I have often done deals which looked good on paper but my instincts told me otherwise. More often than not, after the fact I wished that I had listened to my instincts.

Take some risk

You miss 100% of the shots you don't take.—Wayne Gretzky.
Do I need to say more? Use the "If Then" principle

Goals are necessary but limiting

If you set a goal to run 5 miles then you have achieved your goal and should be proud. But who says that you were not capable of running 10 miles? Sometimes in business you might set a goal to achieve for example sales of $50,000 for the month. You plan your sales calls and resources accordingly. While the setting of the target is necessary, it can also limit you. If you thought that you could sell $80,000 per month, you would not only mentally prepare yourself but you would also plan accordingly. It's not to say that you will achieve sales of $80,000, but one thing's for sure, you will have raised the bar above $50,000 with a reasonable chance of exceeding it. Once you set the goal for $50,000, the chances of exceeding it are minimal. Message: Set goals that may seem unattainable.

Don't get cocky when you win

I have heard my share of sad stories of people who have been successful in relationships or in business and then lost their relationship or business because success went to their head. Conversely I know lots of people who have become super successful and have remained unpretentious and humble. There is no question in my mind that many people who get hurt coming down the mountain do so because they were over confident and perhaps got a little cocky. The mountain identifies the arrogant by taking no prisoners. In business, and in life, nobody wants to hear people show off about their achievements. There is a fine line between cockiness and confidence. Confidence can be advantageous in certain circumstances. But if you have a confident personality you may not know whether you're becoming obnoxious. Try asking people you trust how they perceive you.

Identifying a problem is the first best step to resolving something that may haunt you in the long term. It's tough to undo other people's perceptions of you that have been cemented in their minds. And remember that you make a lasting impression in the first few minutes that you meet them.

It's all in the detail

If you have ever flown in a small aircraft you will understand the word "fear" and what would happen if the plane went down. Responsible pilots know the risk in flying and they also know how to use the "If Then" principle. If my plane loses a rudder or radio then....

I won't bore you with the details but trust me when I tell you that the pre flight check list is extensive and needs to be done EACH AND EVERY TIME he/she flies. There are no ifs or buts. Every part of the check list is completed properly. It's all in the detail.

On 23rd July 1983 Air Canada Flight 143, a Boeing 767 ran out of fuel at 41,000 feet (12,000m) altitude, about halfway through its flight from Montreal to Edmonton. The crew managed to glide the aircraft safely to an emergency landing at Gimli Industrial Park Airport, a former airbase in Manitoba. This was some challenge. No fuel means no engines. No engines means no electronics, no steerage, no navigation. An emergency propeller driven dynamo (similar to that used to produce light on bikes) dropped down on an arm under the plane to produce basic power for steerage. Navigation had to be by sight or calculation of speed etc.

What was the cause of the plane running out of fuel? A simple math error: confusing the units of volume! The fuel requirements were assumed to be in litres but they had been recorded in gallons. Very fortunately the skilled pilots glided the plane down safely with no fatalities. Such a small lack of attention to detail nearly ended in tragedy.

I went into elaborate detail about the necessity for paying close attention to safety using aircraft as the metaphor because I want to make a point.

I mentioned earlier in this book that I have read hundreds of resumés when seeking new employees and it's amazing how many people present resumés with typo's, poor grammar and omitting details that were requested in the advertisement. We disqualify these types of resumés without even looking at their credentials. Why? Because if they are sloppy when presenting themselves, they will be sloppy in their jobs. People who go above and beyond the call of duty to ensure that they look after the small details are the ones who will stand out amongst the crowd. Here is an example of someone I employed because he went the extra mile for his interview.

The job was for a sales professional and we requested him to address us as though we were the customer. He arrived with coffee and pastries for us all. He went out of his way to research both my company and the customer (it was a legitimate potential company that we found on the internet). He must have spent hours preparing a Power Point presentation. He also provided a binder full of materials for each of us. He arrived well on time and wore a nice suit and tie and was clearly very well rehearsed. There were others that we interviewed who may have been a bit more qualified from a technical point of view but he got the job because of his attention to detail and because he had the right attitude. I can teach competence, but it's tough to teach attitude, enthusiasm and commitment.

Life in the balance

Some people will say that hard work never killed anyone but why take the chance!

I am of the opposite opinion. I am now "more senior" and even now still work upward of 50 hours a week. I love what I do and am always seeking new and creative ways to make my job more interesting and fun. When I first started my business I used to work relentlessly 7 days a week . While it was necessary for the first few years it also burned me out. There has to be a balance between hard work, rest and exercise and now that I'm in my later years I have come to realise the merits of balancing all three.

Commitment

I'm not generally big on poetry but every now and then I come across a wonderful poetic verse. I want to share one with you here. It is by an unknown poet and it goes like this:

Don't Quit

When things go wrong as they sometimes will,
When the road you're trudging seems all uphill,
When funds are low and the debts are high,
And you want to smile, but you have to sigh.
When care is pressing you down a bit.
Rest, if you must, but don't you quit.
Life is queer with its twists and turns
As every one of us sometimes learns.
And many a failure turns about
When he might have won had he stuck it out:
Don't give up though the pace seems slow -
You may succeed with another blow.
Success is failure turned inside out -
The silver tint of the clouds of doubt.
And you never can tell how close you are.
It may be near when it seems so far:
So stick to the fight when you're hardest hit
It's when things seem worst that you must not quit.

Thank you for taking the time to read this book. I trust that you have gained insight from these thought provoking ideas, and that you will benefit in your personal or business life.

For more information, or if you want to enter a nice debate with me (I love debating), please feel free to contact me at:

neville@bizwisdom.com

> *Thinking is easy, acting is difficult, and to put one's thoughts into action is the most difficult thing in the world.* —**Goethe**

Notes

Notes

Notes

Notes

NOTES